RATIONAL
CHOICE
THEORY
AND
ORGANIZATIONAL
THEORY:
A CRITIQUE

To Steve Murdock,
one who is truly committed
to fair and equal opportunity
and treatment for all that does not stop
at the conventional lines
of gender, race, and poverty

RATIONAL CHOICE THEORY AND ORGANIZATIONAL THEORY: A CRITIQUE

Mary Zey

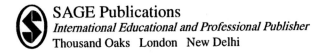

SAGE Publications
International Educational and Professional Publisher
Thousand Oaks   London   New Delhi

For information:

SAGE Publications, Inc.
2455 Teller Road
Thousand Oaks, California 91320
E-mail: order@sagepub.com

SAGE Publications Ltd.
6 Bonhill Street
London EC2A 4PU
United Kingdom

SAGE Publications India Pvt. Ltd.
M-32 Market
Greater Kailash I
New Delhi 110 048 India

Printed in the United States of America

Library of Congress Cataloging-in-Publication Data

Zey, Mary
    Rational choice theory and organizational theory: A critique /
    by Mary Zey.
        p. cm.
    Includes bibliographical references and index.
    ISBN 0-8039-5135-3 (cloth: acid-free paper). —
    ISBN 0-8039-5136-1 (pbk.: acid-free paper)
        1. Rational choice theory. 2. Economic man. 3. Organizational
    sociology. I. Title.
    HB846.8.Z49 1998
    153.8'3—dc21   97-33748

This book is printed on acid-free paper.

98 99 00 01 02 03 10 9 8 7 6 5 4 3 2 1

Acquiring Editor: Harry Briggs
Editorial Assistant: Anna Howland
Production Editor: Sanford Robinson
Production Assistant: Karen Wiley
Book Designer/Typesetter: Janelle LeMaster
Cover Designer: Candice Harman
Print Buyer: Anna Chin

Contents

Preface

I am an organizational sociologist, trained in economic sociology and structural contingency theory at the University of Wisconsin—Madison. For more than two decades, I have benefitted from the teachings and friendships of Michael Aiken, Eric Olin Wright, and Richard Schoenherr, who died prematurely in 1995. From interaction with these structural contingency theorists and neo-Marxists, I developed my political economy contingency model of organizational analysis in the early 1980s with the assistance of Michael Aiken. I have been writing from this perspective for more than two decades.

My objective when I began this book in the early 1980s was to advance the study of macro-organizational theory, which draws upon the sociological and management traditions. These traditions view the organization as the unit of analysis and focus on the relationships of the organization to entities within and external to the organization.

This volume is part of a larger program in which I argue for the empirical validity of structural change of organizations as dependent on the political-legal and economic factors in their environment, including change in capital, the state, and competing and supporting organizations. My position has involved arguing against the more conservative functional sociologists, the more liberal economic theorists of the agency theory, institutional economic transaction cost theory, and for capital dependency theory.

This book has developed over a long period. It began to take form shortly after I began studying and presenting papers in the 1980s about then-evolving fraud networks established by Michael Milken, Ivan Boesky, and various sellers and buyers of junk bonds. In several academic settings, I was faced with shout-downs by organizational economists, who based their objections on the premise that insider trading and securities fraud *should not* be against the law, and that these actors were merely acting rationally. These scholars, newly socialized as organizational economists, could not understand that the premises from which I was working differed from their premises. In fact, they could not see that organizational entities have any real existence beyond that of benefiting their owners or stockholders.

This book is written in response to the neoclassical economic rational choice theories and the organizational economic theories, which have developed in the past decade and which have gained center stage in current organizational analysis.

Acknowledgments

I would like to express my gratitude to Dr. William Perry, Dean of Faculties at Texas A&M University, who provided me with a semester of faculty leave in the fall of 1996 to recollect data and, unknown to him, complete this book. His support has been of great help to me during this time.

I would also like to thank Eric Olin Wright for allowing me to attend his graduate seminar in economic sociology at the University of Wisconsin—Madison in the spring of 1996 and to experience for a second time, a decade later, his excellent lectures. In addition, I would like to thank Jane Pillivan for providing a third opportunity for me to enjoy the stimulating environment of the University of Wisconsin —Madison sociology department.

Some five years ago, in 1991, I was a Visiting Scholar in the Stanford Center for Organizations Research (SCOR). My mentoring host was Dick Scott. Both he and James March asked me to present working draft chapters of my *Banking on Fraud* book in their seminars. Dick Scott was chairing a research seminar on organizations in the Department of Sociology in which the faculty of the department, including John Meyer, and their graduate students were presenting their work. I also participated in the Scandinavian Consortium for Organizations Research seminar, chaired by James March, during which he and his graduate students critiqued my work. I received comments on my work and discussed it with Jeffery Pfeffer, Robert Sutton, and Joel Podolny. I am indebted to them for the lunch discussions about the intellectual diversity in the foundations of management theory and for their support of my research.

During my semester at Stanford, I enjoyed the company of a number of other visiting scholars who assisted me in locating the appropriate library in which to collect financial data for my study of the transformation in corporate form in the 1980s (Zey and Camp 1996 and Zey forthcoming) and who provided intellectual stimulation on a daily basis. Lex Donaldson was my constant intellectual antagonist, strongest critic, and friend, as well as my informant about the development of managerial theory. For his friendship and support, I am deeply grateful.

For their typing and editing, respectfully, the drafts of this manuscript, I would like to thank Charla Adkins and Maveret McClellan. Without their support and friendship, this book would have never been completed. Most important, I would like to thank Harry Briggs, who has supported my work for nearly a decade and, as my editor, flew from California to Texas A&M University in the fall of 1996 and strongly encouraged me to finish this book. His undying support and encouragement have sustained me through the writing of this book as well as my previous book with Sage Publications, *Decision Making: Alternatives to Rational Choice Models* (Zey 1992).

CHAPTER 1

Introduction

What Is Rational Choice Theory?

Although the term *rational choice* is common within the lexicon of many disciplines, there is no clear and distinct set of criteria for delimiting the axiomatic tenets of this theory that is accepted as canonical. The rational choice approach is variously labeled by political scientists as "public choice," by economists as "neoclassicism" and "rational choice theory," by psychologists as "expected utility theory," and by sociologists as "rational choice theory."

The assumptions of rational choice models lie at the heart of modern economic theories of organizations and political doctrines that advocate minimal government, such as libertarianism and anarchism. The assumption is that if individuals behave rationally, the collective will benefit; therefore, individuals should not be interfered with by the collective, except when individual behavior undermines collective interests.

1

The basic principals of rational choice theory (RCT) are derived from neoclassical economic theory, utilitarian theory, and game theory (Levi et al. 1990). The fundamental core of RCT (see Coleman 1990:13-19, 27-44; Friedman and Hechter 1988) is that social interaction is basically an economic transaction that is guided in its course by the actor's rational choices among alternative outcomes. An action is taken only after its benefits and costs have been weighed. The unit of analysis is the individual decision made by an individual decision maker. The individual is purposive and intentional; that is, actors have ends or goals toward which their actions are aimed. The individual decision maker, rather than dyad, group, or organizational entities, is analyzed. Essentially, an actor will choose an action rationally, based on a hierarchy of preferences (values, utilities), that promises to maximize benefits and minimize costs, or more precisely, that promises a net gain of benefits minus costs, or still more precisely, that promises the highest net benefit to the actor and the highest probability of its occurrence. The values at the basis of preferences do not concern rational choice theorists. What is assumed by rational choice theorists is that actions are undertaken to achieve objectives that are consistent with the actor's preference hierarchy. The substance of these values and their source are irrelevant to RCT.

RCT defines rational actions of rational individuals as occurring under several constraints:

1. Scarcity of resources—actors possess different resources, as well as differential access to resources. Scarcity has been an assumption of action theory constructed from various perspectives from Karl Marx ([1867] 1977) through Talcott Parsons and Edward A. Shils (1951).

2. Opportunity costs—this constraint is related to scarcity of resources— opportunity costs are "those costs associated with forgoing the next most attractive course of action" (Friedman and Hechter 1988:202). If a person's chance of achieving the most attractive end are slight, an actor may choose not to pursue the most highly valued end, especially if the actor's resources are negligible, and if, in striving to achieve that end, the actor jeopardizes chances of achieving the next most valued

end. Thus, individual decision makers are viewed as trying to maximize their benefits, which involves assessing the relationship between the chances of achieving a primary end and what that attempt does for chances of attaining the second-most valued or even third-most valued objective.

3. Institutional norms—these institutional constraints affect both rewards and costs, providing support for and constraints against individual actors through such mechanisms as family norms, policies of schools and other formal organizations, governmental laws, and church commandments.

4. Information is an important constraint to making rational choices. Rational choice models traditionally assume that actors have perfect, or at least sufficient, information to make purposive choices among the alternative courses of action. With new and increasingly sophisticated methods of acquiring information and communicating information, there is growing recognition that lack of quantity is not a problem. However, quality of available information is highly variable, and this variability has profound effects on actors' choices. The ability to control the source, amount, content, and accuracy of information has never been a stronger constraint on rational decision making.

The process by which "individual actions are combined to produce the social outcome" is the aggregation mechanism (Friedman and Hechter 1988:203). RCT does not deal with groups, or collective group behavior, only with the aggregation of individual action.

Major Proponents of
Rational Choice Theory

RCT is a special type of the broader category of exchange theory developed by George Homans, and much later, Peter Blau, and it was central to the development of sociology and organizational theory. RCT became prominent as an explanation of social action largely through the efforts of James S. Coleman in the late 1980s and early 1990s.

In 1989, Coleman founded a journal, *Rationality & Society*, devoted to the dissemination of work by rational choice theorists. In the journal's first issue, under the title "The Paradigm of Rational Action," Coleman (1989) claims that this is the only theory with the possibility of producing paradigmatic integration. Coleman goes on to argue that this paradigm operates from a base of methodological individualism and uses RCT as the microlevel base for the explanation of macrolevel phenomena.

In the following year, Coleman (1990) published *Foundations of Social Theory* based on rational choice propositions, and two years later, he used his 1992 presidential address at the American Sociological Association, "The Rational Reconstruction of Society" (Coleman 1992), to promote this theory further. At that same meeting, he organized two sessions of invited papers to exhort the advantages of RCT. Subsequently, some of these papers were published in an anthology titled *Rational Choice Theory: Advocacy and Critique*, edited by James Coleman and Thomas J. Fararo (1993), which was sympathetically as well as critically reviewed (see Zey 1994).

In addition to criticisms made about what RCT assumes and posits, there are an equal number of criticisms that could be made about what Coleman (1989) has excluded. In his own words, he excludes

> work that is methodologically holistic . . . without recourse to actors whose actions generate that system, . . . the view of action as purely expressive, the view of action as irrational, and also the view of action as something wholly caused by outside forces without the intermediation of intention or purpose. It excludes the empirical work widely carried out in social science in which individual behavior is "explained" by certain factors or determinants without any model of action whatsoever. (p. 6)

Rather than explaining social phenomena by other "social facts" in the tradition of Emile Durkheim ([1895] 1982), Coleman argues that social science should focus on social systems and explain them by internal factors, specifically by individual rational choices. His methodology rests on the assumption that data should be generated at the individual level and then aggregated to yield the system level of analysis. Given his methodological individualism, Coleman focuses on the micro-macro linkage or on how a combination of individual actions brings about the behavior of the system and how individual actions affect other individual actions. Although he notes the importance of the micro-macro linkage through his analysis of constraints, he generally does not analyze the macro to micro linkages. His linkages are one-directional, with little consideration of how social system organizations affect the actions of individuals. Coleman favors the individual level of analysis for paradigmatic reasons. He sees social science not merely as an academic exercise but as a means of "intervention" to create social change. His focus on the individual level provides him easy access to intervene in individual behavior to make changes. He holds that macro, organizational, and societal change come about through individual changes.

Coleman (1990) argues that "persons act purposively toward a goal, with the goal (and thus the actions) shaped by values or preferences" (p. 13). This argument is similar to that of early Parsonsian voluntarianism (Parsons and Shils 1951). Coleman then argues that we need a more precise conceptualization of the rational actor derived from economics, one that views the actor as choosing those actions that maximize utility or satisfy needs and wants. The key elements here are actors and resources. Resources are those things over which actors have control and in which they have some interest. Coleman (1990) describes interaction from his methodological individualist perspective as follows:

> A minimal basis for a social system of action is two actors, each having control over resources of interest to the other. It is each one's interest in resources under the other's control that leads the two, as purposive actors, to engage in actions that involve each other . . . a system of action. (p. 29)

Coleman further demonstrates that he believes that the RCT that he sets forth ultimately can explain all social action. He writes, "Success of a social theory based on rationality lies in successively diminishing that domain of social activity that cannot be accounted for by the theory" (Coleman 1990:18). Various economists have set about this task with great vigor (see Gary Becker 1962, 1968, 1975, 1976, 1981). When individuals do not act rationally, Coleman believes that it makes little difference for the predictability of this theory. He writes, "My implicit assumption is that the theoretical predictions made here will be substantially the same whether the actors act precisely according to rationality as commonly conceived or deviate in the ways that have been observed" (Coleman 1990:506).

A second key concept in the linkages between micro and macro units is the granting of authority and rights possessed by one individual to another. Coleman argues that this linkage creates the basic macro phenomenon, a dyad consisting of two people that is an authority-bound and interdependent acting unit rather than two independent actors. The resulting structure functions independently of the two separate actors. The two actors no longer maximize their independent individual outcomes but, rather, maximize the outcome of the independent collective unit.

How, then, does Coleman conceptualize collective behavior? To him, "collective behavior is a simple (and rational) transfer of control over one's actions to another actor . . . made unilaterally, not as part of an exchange" (Coleman 1990:198). This leads Coleman to the next logical question regarding which people unilaterally transfer control over their actions to others. The answer, from a rational choice perspective, is that it is those people who wish to maximize their utility. Coleman posits that individuals' maximization involves a balancing of control among several actors, and that this produces equilibrium within society. I argue that in the case of collective behavior, because there is a unilateral transfer of control, individual maximization does not lead to system equilibrium.

Major Proponents of the
Convergence of Rational Choice Theory
and Organizational Theory

In the past two decades, economists and organizational theorists have shown increasing interest in the substantive issues that, until recently, were considered the intellectual domain of the other. The population ecology perspective (PE) of organizations, as developed by organizational sociologists Michael T. Hannan and John H. Freeman (Hannan and Freeman 1977; see also Aldrich 1979), is strikingly similar to rational choice economic models in that it makes similar assumptions about the nature of humans, survival of the fittest, and organizational performance. Transaction cost analysis (TCA), developed by an economist, Oliver Williamson,[1] explains why some typically rational market transactions are more efficiently performed by organizations. Human capital theory, as developed by economist Gary Becker (1975), treats issues of status attainment, stratification, inequality, and various organizational decisions, including family size, by using RCT and modeling. Some organizational theorists have become concerned with matters of agency (e.g., Jensen and his associates), whereas others have begun to study markets.[2]

Much that has been written by rational choice theorists places all social, political, and economic behavior under the same premise of competition for scarce goods. James Buchanan and Gordon Tullock (1962) proposed this point of departure: "The representative or average individual acts on the basis of the same over-all values scale when he participates in market activity and in [a] political activity" (p. 20). Subsequently, others have followed their lead in noting that one of the significant accomplishments of RCT is that it led to "a reintegration of politics and economics under a common paradigm and deductive structure" (Ordeshook 1993:76).

Others have carried the accolades even further to claim that the use of RCT accounts for the only "genuine advances ever to occur in [social] political science" (Riker 1990:177-78). Jack Knight (1992) asserts that RCT "has significantly advanced our understanding of the role of institutions of social life" (p. 1063), and Kristen Monroe (1991b) touts rational choice as "one of the dominant paradigms of political and social science, offering insightful, rigorous and parsimonious explanations" (p. 2). Peter Abell (1992) concurs and encourages sociologists to adopt RCT because of its achievement in political science, which is, according to his assessment, "barely necessary to mention" (pp. 203-204). Like economists, political scientists and sociologists appeal to deductive, ad hoc accounts of incentives, constraints, and calculation to explain social action. Those who hold the rational choice perspective claim that sociology and political science have not adequately studied the microfoundation of social behavior. In fact, RCT reduces social behavior to individual actions. Organizational, collective, and group behavior are reduced to individual action and individual calculus. Thus, the behavior of corporations, party behavior, policy making, strategies, and social structures are reduced to the same individual unit of analysis as the single voter and consumer. According to RCT, the social sciences have simply studied the right phenomena in the wrong way.

As Gary Becker (1981) points out,

> The economic approach is not restricted to material goods and wants or to markets with monetary transactions, and *conceptually* does not distinguish between major and minor decisions or between "emotional" or other decisions. Indeed . . . the economic approach provides a framework applicable to all human behavior—to all types of decisions and to persons from all walks of life. (p. ix)[3]

In spite of such sweeping statements, the convergence between rational choice neoclassical economic theory and organizational theory is more apparent than real. Although both theories analyze the same substantive areas, they do not ask the same questions, use the same assumptions, or develop the same hypotheses and theories. Because of their largely different intellectual traditions and worldviews, they are not able to be integrated into a single theory. Yet in recent years, RCT has been extended in application to social phenomena outside the purely economic realm to relationships that are core to organizational analysis. As such, RCT has attained the position of a paradigm that has been claimed to function as a core for theorizing about organizations as a whole, as, for example, *in the theory of the firm*.

In Coleman's (1990) *Foundations of Social Theory*, RCT has been advocated as having a potential for synthesizing sociological theory from a great variety of approaches. To do this, RCT must explain some of the following relationships: power, conflict, trust, solidarity, inequality (especially information and knowledge inequities), organizational actions, communication, and legitimacy.

Over the past two decades, political science, like sociology, has experienced a movement toward RCT. In 1994, Donald P. Green and Ian Shapiro published a critical analysis of work done by political scientists who applied the rational choice perspective to empirical studies. *Pathologies of Rational Choice Theory* focuses on the lack of correspondence between the rational choice model and the actual political phenomena that it is used to model.

Advocates of RCT wrote scathing reviews and responses to Green and Shapiro that were collected by Critical Review Foundation and published in *Critical Review* in 1995. The following year, Yale University Press published a revised edition that was edited by Jeffrey Friedman and titled *The Rational Choice Controversy*. The concluding chapter of this volume is Green and Shapiro's response to criticism of their work made by Friedman and his associates. As a result of this exchange, the lack of fit between the rational choice model and social and political collective actions has come under intense scrutiny in the past several years.

RCT exemplifies a highly abstract, deductive approach characterized by the development of models based on deliberately, rigidly simplified assumptions. These models are elegant and parsimonious to ensure accurate prediction. The individual level of analysis is taken to real and higher levels (group, organizations, and interorganizational networks) as derived and built on the individual level through aggregation. Heuristic assumptions about human nature include that humans are basically greedy and self-interested with fixed hierarchical preferences. Assumptions about social systems are that the preexisting state of social orders is scarcity, and the preeminence of markets is given and is unquestioned in the development of principles and models.

In contrast, organizational analysis tends to value description and explanation over prediction. The extent to which the theory corresponds to the real world is paramount, and the resemblance of the theory to the perceptions and meanings of participants and observers is highly valued. There are few, if any, fundamental assumptions in organizational theory. Even rationality of human action and organizational rationality are challenged. Furthermore, there is no single, widely accepted worldview (paradigm) in organizational analysis, either theoretical or methodological. Organizational analysis is more empirical and data driven than rational choice analysis; that is, organizational analysts spend much more time gathering original data, analyzing it, and interpreting it than they do in model building.

The important question to which this book speaks is, *Given the well-established differences between rational choice and organizational theories, what are the limits of fruitful dialogue and collaboration between the two fields?* The concepts and assumptions of rational action—for example, the acceptance of the individual as the unit of analysis as the "real and only" level of analysis, and the deductive (and often highly mathematical) style of theorizing based on the operation of these actors under conditions of scarcity, along with a related set of assumptions about human nature—are currently influencing the field of organizations. Although organizational theorists take organizations and the greater society as their unit of analysis, they seem increasingly enamored of RCT and methods.

Conclusion

RCT thus sees human action primarily in economic terms and is not concerned with the ethics or values that lead to rational decisions. Although action is constrained by a variety of circumstances, these circumstances and the resulting collective actions are not analyzed. Social outcomes are produced by individual actions that are aggregated and are explained without reference to other social facts. People give up autonomy only if by doing so they maximize benefit to themselves. Because all are maximizing in relation to all others, a natural equilibrium in the system is achieved. RCT claims to be able to explain noneconomic social phenomena but does not adequately address issues such as power, trust, communication, and solidarity. This is a formal, rigid theory that achieves a high degree of predictability because it is self-referential and brushes aside instances of nonrational behavior, such as altruism. The very concept of rationality itself is used in a narrow and particular way.

Notes

1. Oliver Williamson published *Markets and Hierarchies* in 1975. In the past two decades, his theory has been expanded by others, such as Jay B. Barney and William G. Ouchi (1986).
2. See Wayne Baker's analysis of the futures market (Baker 1983, 1989), as well as Mary Zey's (1993) analysis of the high-yield bond market.
3. For an even stronger statement of this imperialist stance, see also George Stigler and Gary Becker (1977).

CHAPTER 2

Individual Rationality versus Collective Rationality

My purpose in this chapter is to differentiate between individual and collective rationality and to describe the rational choice approach to the study of organizations. In addition, I hope to provide an understanding of the major ways that rationality has been characterized in the rational choice tradition and the significance this description has had for rational choice theory (RCT) and its empirical testing.

It seems clear that some premises of RCT are generally shared and therefore meet the test of consensus, and thus are noncontroversial. They are as follows:

1. Utility is maximized.

2. Preferences are structured.

3. Decisions are made under conditions of uncertainty.

4. Individuals are the unit of analysis and individual behavior is central to our understanding of organizations, not norms, positions, power, class, or status.

The connotations of the term *rational* range from "formal notions of efficiency and consistency to the substantive notions of autonomy and self-determination" (Elster 1983:1). Rationality, as Elster (1983) notes, has been applied to many concepts: "beliefs, preferences, choices or decisions, actions, behavioral patterns, persons, even collectives and institutions" (p. 1).

One common meaning of rationality is "reasoned action" of any type. Another common meaning is that "one is rational if, after considering all of one's concerns—moral, altruistic, familial, narrowly self-interested, and so forth—one then chooses coherently in trading each off against the other, or even in refusing to make certain trade-offs" (Hardin 1982:10). Another meaning of rationality that is used by Russell Hardin (1982) is that rational means "efficient in securing one's self-interest" (p. 10). As Hardin points out, at issue is the extent to which this even more narrowly defined rational behavior affects outcomes in social collectives, such as groups and organizations.

The earliest economic theorists defined rationality only as "self-interest." For example, Adam Smith, in *The Wealth of Nations* ([1776] 1979) argues that

individuals contribute to the general productiveness of society although their intent is to be only interested in their own gain. This action is led, as in many other cases, by an invisible hand to promote an end which was no part of his intention. . . . By pursuing his own interest he frequently promotes that of society more effectually than when he really intends to promote it. (p. 426)

In other words, Adam Smith defines collective interest as being served as each person serves his or her own self-interest. Under capitalism, individuals live well because some seek to profit from providing the goods and services that others want or prefer, and society benefits as an accidental consequence of each individual's self-interested choices, decisions, and actions.

Russell Hardin, in *Collective Action* (1982) argues in contrast to Adam Smith that we are often less helped by the benevolent invisible hand of capitalism (which is disrupted by state intervention) than "we are injured by the malevolent back of that hand; that is, in seeking private interests, we fail to secure greater collective interests" (p. 6). The cost of being at "the back of the hand" has been argued by many over the past 30 years, from 1976, when Mancur Olson's ([1965] 1971) *The Logic of Collective Action* was republished, to today's analyses of such collective actions as the prisoner's dilemma, free riders, common fate, and others.

The conclusion that collective action is based on the strong but narrow assumption that individual actions are motivated by self-interest not only forms the basis for past theories but for contemporary theories of organizations such as agency and transaction cost economics. Although these same theorists hold that it is obvious that individual actions are sometimes motivated by concerns in addition to self-interest, the collective action of a group or organization is conceived as narrowly rational. Thus, many who want their collective interests to be served may hold that their own self-interests are more important—so important, in fact, that cooperation in serving collective interests through collective action is overridden.

Individual Rationality

While acknowledging that a fuller theory is needed to account for the "moral worth of the person" (Rawls 1971:397), Donald Davidson (1980) explains rational action as action that stands in a certain relation to the agent's beliefs and desires. Because RCT does not scrutinize the fundamental bases of the reasons for actions taken, it is considered thin. Davidson (1980) holds that we must require, first, that the reasons are reasons for the action; second, that the reasons do, in fact, cause the action for which they are reasons; and third, that the reasons cause the action "in the right way." Elster (1983) argues:

> Implicit in these requirements is also a consistency requirement for the desires and beliefs themselves. In what follows, the focus will mainly be on consistency, but first I have a few words to say about the three clauses that went into the definition of rational action. (p. 3)

With regard to this formal/thin rationality, the stipulation is made that beliefs and desires must not be logically inconsistent with actions. According to Elster (1983), "Consistency is what rationality in the thin sense is all about; consistency within the belief system; consistency within the system of desires; and between beliefs and desires" (p. 1) and between the related actions that they cause. As an alternative explanation, see Weber's four bases of action: tradition, affect, rational-legal, and substantively rational action.

Rawls argues that a view of "the good" must rest at the basis of a notion of rationality, and that a view of "goodness" must be used to defend justice as fairness. Rawls (1971:397) posits that a person may know so little about a situation that a rational agreement upon principles is impossible. However, the "thin theory of good" would hold

> that the rationality of a person's choice does not depend upon how much he knows, but only upon how well he reasons from whatever information he has, however incomplete. . . . The thin theory of the good which the parties are assumed to accept shows that they should try to secure their liberty and self-respect, and that, in order to advance their aims, whatever these are, they normally require more rather than less of the other primary goods. . . . [We] need what I have called the thin theory of the good to explain the rational preference for primary good and to explicate the notion of rationality underlying the choice of principles in the original position. This theory is necessary to support the requisite premises from which the principles of justice are de-

rived. . . . [However,] a more comprehensive account of the good is essential. (Rawls 1971:397)

Collective Rationality

Rational choice theorists, other than those who study collective rationalization, generally assume that the relevant maximizing agents are individuals, not classes, groups, departments, or other social entities. It is by reference to the maximizing actions of individuals that collective action and outcomes are explained. For example, Buchanan and Tullock (1962) hold that collective action is no more than aggregate individual action. Riots, revolts, and other mob activities are engaged in by separate, rational, individual actors who have preferences. Societies, organizations, and mobs do not have preference orders as do individuals. Several rational choice theorists hold that because mechanisms through which rational choice explanation operate are the preferences and beliefs of individuals, rational choice explanations cannot be predicated upon anything other than individual preferences. Rational choice is about the business of explaining collective actions and outcomes on the basis of individual behavior.

In the rational choice tradition, the formal rationality of decision making can be attributed to collective decision making (in political science, social choice theory) or to the aggregate outcome of individual decisions. In both cases, individual desires are preferences that are taken as given, and rationality is defined mainly as a relation between preferences measured as behavior and social outcomes. In contrast, according to Elster (1983), a broader theory of collective rationality deals with the "capacity of the social system or the collective decision mechanism to bring the individual preferences into line with the broad notion of individual rationality" (p. 2). Substantively, collective rationality controls autonomous desires.

What makes collective rationality "collective"? Agreeing with Elster, I argue that collective rationality is not individual preferences aggregated, nor is it the censoring of preferences. Rather, collective rationality is the result of public and rational dialogue about the common good. In the political realm, a reasonable outcome is more likely when preferences are transformed, not when they are aggregated. The goal of politics should be unanimous and thoughtful consensus, not an optimal compromise between irreducibly opposed interests. Furthermore, the quintessential element of the political process is the collective forging of a decision, not the individual exercising his or her right to vote.

Elster (1983) establishes two premises for collective action. First, "there are certain arguments that simply cannot be stated publicly in a political setting. In political discussion it is pragmatically impossible to assert that a given solution be chosen simply because it favors oneself" (p. 35) or one's group. One can bargain for oneself but cannot argue for oneself alone. Women and minorities

> cannot claim advantages simply by virtue of their status. They must argue that the status entitles them to advantages because of certain ethically relevant features that, if found in other groups as well, would entitle the members to similar benefits. To argue on grounds of entitlement, rather than simply negotiating from strength, logically implies readiness to accept the claims of others (p. 35)

who have similar entitlements.

The second premise is that, over time, one who pays lip service to the common good will come to be persuaded by the common good. This is a psychological rather than a conceptual premise. Elster (1983) holds that one would have to invoke the power of reason to break down prejudice and selfishness. By speaking in the voice of reason, one also exposes oneself to the effects of reason. Because one cannot argue for the good of others without eventually believing the arguments, and because it is not at all acceptable to argue only for one's own good, Elster (1983) maintains that public discussions must lead to realization of the common good. The *volonte generale*, then, will not simply be the Pareto-optimal realization of given (or expressed) preferences, but the emergence of preferences that are themselves shaped by concern for the common good. (p. 36)

Irrationality

One superficial way to look at irrationality is to say that rationality informs the agent as to what to do; *if the actor behaves otherwise, then he or she is irrational.* Elster (1983) argues that there are many cases in which rationality "can do no more than exclude certain alternatives, while not providing any guide to the choice between the remaining" (p. 2) alternatives. Here, Elster relies on higher levels of information as he posits that "if we want to *explain* behavior in such cases, causal considerations must be invoked in addition to the assumption of rationality" (p. 2). In fact, causal considerations are what Elster defines as the broader (thicker) type of rationality.

Rational action, then, is action that stands in a certain relation to the agent's beliefs and desires (which Elster refers to as the agent's *reasons*). However, three criteria are necessary here: (1) "that the reasons are reasons for action"; (2) that the reasons do, in fact, cause the action for which they are reasons; and (3) "that the reasons cause the actions in the intended way." In this way, desires or preferences, beliefs, and actions are consistent. Elster (1983) demonstrates how extremely thin this definition of rationality is with the following example: "If an agent has a compulsive desire to kill another person, and believes that the best way (or a way) of killing that person is to stick a pin through a doll representing him, then he acts rationally if he sticks a pin through the doll" (p. 3). Elster then accurately points out that there are few who would accept the substantive rationality of that desire and that belief, and even fewer who would hold that the action is substantively rational even if the desires and beliefs are held. Neither point 2 nor point 3 is fulfilled by the example. Thus, point 1 is not connected to points 2 or 3.

The second point—that the reasons do, in fact, cause the action—is necessary because a person may act because of factors other than his or her reason for acting. For example, a person could do inadvertently what he or she in fact has a reason for doing. One may act out of emotion, tradition, compulsion, or inclinations other than reason. Here, the reasons do not cause the actions; therefore, they are not rational.

The third point is that the reasons do, in fact, cause the action for which they are reasons, but according to Elster (1983), they do so in the wrong way. Davidson (1980, chap. 2) coins the term, *non-standard causal chains*. The example given by Davidson is, "A man may try to kill someone by shooting at him. Suppose the killer misses his victim by a mile, but the shot stampedes a herd of wild pigs that trample the intended victim to death" (p. 78). Elster (1983) argues that "we do not want to say that the man killed the victim intentionally, since the causal chain is of the wrong kind" (p. 9), not what the man intended. The beliefs and desires are consistent with the action, but the causal chain is missing; something else happened over which the actor had little or no control. The means were not those intended, although the end was quite desirable.

Individuals are taken to have rational preferences if (1) their preferences are complete and transitive, and to choose rationally if their preferences are rational; and (2) there is no feasible option that they could prefer to the chosen option. Preferences are complete if, for all instances of options A and B, the individual prefers A to B, or B to A, or is indifferent between A and B. The individual's preferences are transitive if, for all options A, B, and C, the person prefers A to B and B to C; then this person can be said to prefer A to C. If the person is indifferent to A and B, and B and C, then the person is indifferent between A and C.

In the theory of rational choice, preferences must be both complete and consistent; that is, one must be either indifferent to one element in a set of two choices, or prefer one of them over the other. Elster (1983) argues that "there is no strong argument for consistency. In fact, one could argue that it is irrational to commit oneself to a preference for one of the options if one knows very little about either" (p. 8). Thus, what is appropriate for powerful model building—a complete transitive, continuous, and stable ordering of all possible preferences—may be unrealistic. He goes on to point out that "for model building purposes, however, the condition is very important, since preferences that are transitive, complete and continuous can be represented by a real-valued *utility function*" (p. 9).

Utility Maximization

In modern utility theory, the phrase "maximize utility" is essentially shorthand for preferences and implies nothing about more or less pleasurable mental states that could be seen as the goal of behavior as originally defined by Jeremy Bentham ([1841] 1983). To maximize utility is not to engage in the carrying out of a plan, choosing the best means to realize an independently defined end. Utility maximization is *not* maximization of pleasure, happiness, or satisfaction. Elster (1983) makes the accurate point that

> even if one should succeed in defining a cardinal measure of utility [satisfaction], it would be a mistake to believe that action could then always be explained in terms of utility maximization in the same sense as, say, investment may be explained in terms of profit maximization, (p. 9)

as a plan undertaken as a conscious and deliberate attempt to maximize utility (pleasure/satisfaction/happiness). Such plans tend to be self-defeating. Elster points out that "it is a truism, and an important one, that happiness tends to elude those who actively strive for it" (p. 9).

Economists typically take the existence of "rational preferences as tantamount to the existence of a *utility function* and rational choice as utility maximization" (Hausman 1992:18). However, the existence of a real-valued utility function also requires that preferences be, in a specific sense, continuous. The question arises, Must an individual be able to rank all feasible options, or is it enough that an individual be able to rank all the options that are available in the given context or under a given set of circumstances? All of this confusion has led many economists to eliminate references to subjective preferences, and to theorize instead in terms of choices only. Thus, there is no attempt to make the connection between subjectively rational preferences and objectively rational choice of preferences.

Completeness (comparability of options or connectedness or connectivity of preferences) states that individuals can compare all options. Completeness is an idealization; most humans have no set ranking of the numerous and complex options that exist. Many neither know what their choices would be, nor do they care. In any case, to argue that completeness is possible under conditions of certainty is irrelevant, because conditions are seldom certain.

In summary, the *ordinal representation theorem* states that if an individual's preferences are complete, transitive, and continuous, then they may be represented by a continuous real-value utility function (Debreu 1959:54-9). The number assigned to each option tells us how highly ranked the option is—the higher the number, the more preferred the option. The utility function is limited; it is measured only at an ordinal level, not an internal level. Thus, absolute magnitudes, sums, and differences are arbitrary (Hausman 1992:19).

When economists say that individuals maximize utility, they are only saying that people do not rank any feasible option above the option they choose. Utility is an index of preferences according to most economic theory. An individual who is a utility maximizer just does what he or she most prefers. To say that someone maximizes utility says nothing about the substantive nature of the preferences held.

Utility Theory Is a Normative
and a Rational Theory

Utility maximization is the assumption that when decision makers are confronted with options, they will pick the one that best serves their objectives. The actions of a group or a person are rational when objectives are pursued "by means that are efficient for achieving these objectives" given their preferences (Olson [1965] 1971:65). The maximization assumption requires only that some schedule of preferences exists. No particular goal is defined within this assumption.

Utility theory is both normative and positivistic. What makes utility theory primarily a normative theory is the fact that rationality is a normative notion—a notion based on what *should* or *ought* to be. To define rational preferences and choices is to say how one ought rationally to prefer and to choose. It should be noted, however, that not everyone would accept this description, most notably economic theorists. Utility theory may also be positivistic in that it not only defines what ought to be, but claims that people are rational in the sense defined. Utility theory, as a positivistic theory of preference and choice, is crucial to RCT. Utility theory says nothing about what people desire, want, or prefer. It only requires consistency of preferences and that choices manifest preferences. It says nothing specifically about commodities or services, efficiency or effectiveness, or other goals. Utility theory has nonnormative elements in that it says nothing about whether a person is acquisitive, self-interested, or other-interested, or whether a person is good or evil.

The Assumption of Context Independence
and the Context-Dependent Organization

Although economists may prefer not to theorize about context or simply assume it away, preferences are context dependent. In one situation, a person may prefer A to B and choose A, thus making a rational decision based on consistency. However, in another situation, the same person may choose between A, B, and C, and chooses B to C, and C to A, and B to A; therefore, in this situation, the choices are consistent and rational based on the consistency principal. Indeed, in the second situation, the person's preferences are complete and transitive, and the choices are rational. But, in combining situation 1 and situation 2, the choices seem quite inconsistent. The preferences and choices in one interaction situation are not consistent with those in the other, and from the perspective of RCT, the actions together are not rational. A possible explanation is that the two situations are separated in time, and that over time, the person's preferences, and therefore choices, have changed. If time has not changed and the individual's preferences or the time frame is the same, it is likely that the preference for relationship between A and B is dependent on the presence of C. That is, the interaction between C and A changes the individual's rank of preferences to place B over A in the presence of C. Situational context is important; however, rational choice models do not usually theorize about the relationship between the context and nonrational action.

This is the crux of the problem of applying microeconomic theory to organizational analysis. Context and conditions are constantly changing, and the mix of individuals and conditions vary from one interaction frame to the next. Because the context-independent assumption at the basis of economic theories is hidden, when applied to organizational analysis, it becomes, in important ways, more demanding than the requirement of completeness and transitivity of preferences. The reason for this is that organizations are open systems with constant feedback from the external environment; this means that the opportunities and constraints provided by the environment are constantly changing, and the mix is never stable. Organizational decision makers do not make context-independent decisions because the nature of their existence is context dependent, not context independent. That is, individuals depend on their physical, economic, and political environments when they make decisions.

RATIONAL MAN VERSUS ECONOMIC (SELFISH) MAN

Rational man is that person we described above as having only consistent preferences that lead to consistent actions. Economic man is a more ideal person possessing much more highly endowed character. He has "preferences that are not only consistent, but also complete, continuous and *selfish*" (Elster 1983:10). Economists derive all apparently nonselfish behavior from selfish preferences (Axelrod and Hamilton 1981). Elster (1983) describes the latitude that this premise provides to economists' research strategies when they explain behavior, in that they "assume first that it is selfish; if not then at least rational; if not, then at least intentional" (p. 10). All forms of altruism, solidarity, and sacrifice really are ultra-subtle forms of self-interest.

OPTIMALITY OF RATIONAL BEHAVIOR

Ideas about the best way to realize one's desires deal with the unicity[1] and optimality of rational behavior. To maximize some objective or realize some plan in the best way necessitates the distinction of various forms of maximizing behavior. Maximizing requires information concerning the nature of the environment and the extent to which it is known to the agent. Environments, from the perspective of the decision maker, range from passive to active and strategic, and on the second characteristic, from certain to uncertain and risky.

Under conditions of certainty, the basic model of choice implicit in standard microeconomic theory is that an agent's choice or action is the result of that person's beliefs and preferences. Choice is rational when it is determined by rational beliefs and preferences. Economists have relatively little to say about rational beliefs.

Individuals are taken to have perfect knowledge. However, in the real world, the uncertainty of incomplete knowledge cannot be avoided. Problems arise when it is necessary to say something about beliefs and preferences under conditions of uncertainty. *The major question is, Which beliefs and preferences are rational under conditions of uncertainty?*

		Conditions	
		Certainty	Uncertainty/Risk
Environment	Passive	1	2
	Active/Strategic	3	4

Preferences refer to the subjective state of individuals, which is reflected in their words and actions, whereas choice is ambiguous between subjective deliberation and its consequent action. Hausman (1992:14) defines "preferences to be subjective states for which choices, construed as actions, provide fallible evidence." The standard problem of optimization is located in cell 1, when the environment is both certain and passive. Under these conditions, there may be several options that are equally maximally good (Ullmann-Margalit 1977), according to the chosen objective.

In the case of a passive environment under conditions of uncertainty or risk, the maximal becomes the expected value of the objective function, or some modification thereof, "and accounts for risk aversion and irreversibility" (Elster 1983:12). Assuming that there are cases in which there is genuine uncertainty or ignorance, Elster (1983), following Arrow and Hurwicz (1972), argues that we are unable to attach any numerical probabilities to the possible outcomes of action in these cases. Under conditions of uncertainty due to ignorance, "we know that rationally one can take account only of the best and worst consequences attached to each course of action" (p. 12). If a decision maker can choose only the best consequence, "it follows that neither unicity nor optimality will obtain" (p. 13).

If the environment is active or uncertain rather then passive, Elster (1983) moves immediately to the assumptions that govern game theory.

1. The reward of each depends on the reward of all, through envy, altruism, etc.
2. The reward of each depends on the action of all, through general social causality.
3. The action of each depends on the actions of all, by strategic reasoning.
4. The desires of each depend on the action of all. This refers to the fact that individual preferences and plans are social in their origin, which differs from the idea that they may be social in their scope, i.e. that the welfare of others may be part of the goal of the individual....

Interdependency of choices turns on the notion of an *equilibrium point*; a set of strategies that are optimal against each other. (p. 13)

Rationality, Utility Theory, and Choice

THE NORMATIVE DIMENSION AND
THE GENERALIZATION OF INDIVIDUAL
BEHAVIOR TO THE COLLECTIVE

Economists portray individuals as choosing rationally. They offer generalizations concerning how people make choices and claim that this is how agents (in the interest of principals) *ought to choose*. Some economists argue that the normative plausibility of the view of rationality implicit in economics is irrelevant to empirical assessment, which affords them the opportunity to ignore this normative assumption by first assuming it and then assuming it does not exist.

What is it to choose rationally? Economists regard choice as arising from preferences (desires) and expectations (beliefs). Economists take preferences as givens that are not subject to rational appraisal or worthy of empirical verification. However, preferences and beliefs may be nonrational, or even irrational based on the criterion of consistency (Elster 1983; Hausman 1992).

REVEALED PREFERENCES THEORY

Rational choice theorists assume that social actions and out-comes are the consequences of individual choices and that they correspond to individual intentions. According to Debra Satz and John Ferejohn (1993:1-2), this is a psychological assumption that has been combined with the highly reductionist RCT, where the behavior of the social collective is explained in terms of the desires and beliefs of its individuals.

In an attempt to escape the question of whether preferences and choices are consistent, revealed preferences have been touted as the appropriate alternative to consistency between the subjective and action. The basic idea of revealed preference theory is that if a person chooses option A when he or she might have chosen B or C, then A is revealed to be preferred. The person's preferences are consistent if they satisfy the so-called *"weak axiom of revealed preference."* Thus, if A is revealed to be preferred to B, then B must not be revealed as preferred to A. In this model, *choice demonstrates preference.* The causal relation is from the action to the subjective. They are one and the same. If choice is a proxy for preference, then preference and choice cannot be demonstrated empirically to be inconsistent. The assumption of revealed preferences as a basis for choice is limited in that it impoverishes both the normative theory of rationality and the empirical theory of choice. Completeness, the relationship between preferences and choices, cannot even be broached within a revealed-preference approach—nor can the question of whether individuals may sometimes choose (perhaps for moral reasons) something that they do not prefer (Sen 1977). One cannot answer the questions of how and why changed preferences affect actions (Hirschman 1985) because actions are preferences.

In explaining why the conception of man in economic models tends to be that of a self-seeking egoist through revealed preference theory, Sen (1977) writes, "It is possible to define a person's interests in such a way that no matter what he does he can be seen to be furthering his own interests in every isolated act of choice" (p. 322). The reduction of man to a self-seeking animal depends in this approach on careful definition and theorizing. If an individual is observed to choose A while rejecting B, he or she has revealed a preference of A over B. His or her personal utility is then defined as simply a numerical representation of this "preference," assigning a higher utility to a "preferred" alternative. With this definition, one can escape maximizing one's utility only through inconsistency. Thus if this individual chooses B over A on the next occasion under the same conditions, the revealed preference theorist cannot label the individual as utilitarian and maximizing. The individual is either inconsistent, or else his or her preferences are changing. Sen cleverly points out,

> But if you are consistent, then no matter whether you are a single-minded egoist or a raving altruist or a class conscious militant, you will appear to be maximizing your own utility in this enchanted world of definition. Borrowing from the terminology used in connection with taxation, if the Arrow-Hahn justification of the assumption of egoism amounts to the *avoidance* of the issue, the revealed preference approach looks more like a robust piece of *evasion*. (p. 323)

For Sen (1973), the approach of definitional egoism sometimes masquerades as rational choice, which means nothing more than internal consistency. A person's choice can be considered rational if and only if these choices can all be explained in terms of some preference relation consistent with the revealed preference definition, that is, if all of his or her choices can be explained as the choosing of "most preferred" alternatives with respect to a postulated preference relation. The limitation is that the only way of understanding a person's real preference is to examine his or her actual choices, and there is no choice-independent way of understanding someone's attitude toward alternatives. Behavior is behavior, and behavior is revealed in revealed preference theory.

Sen (1973:242-244) also makes the point that the sense of revealed preference theory remains parasitic on the subjective notion of preference that it supposedly eschews. Social scientists are interested in choices, which implies that human actions are intentional rather than some predetermined reflex. The implications of these assumptions are discarded by revealed preference theory. Furthermore, this assumption of revealed preference theory, when applied to organizational analysis, is erroneous on at least two grounds. First, revealed preferences will show intransitivities under conditions of risk and uncertainty that have nothing to do with "irrationality" as defined by RCT. Second, in organizations, one may choose action B, even when he or she prefers A, as a strategic move to hide something, mislead others, or manipulate the choice mechanisms in some way.

In summary, little can be said in support of revealed preference theory because its purported empirical advantages are negligible, and it impoverishes the theory of choice by presupposing the subjective notions it attempts to avoid.

Empirical Tests

Only rarely does RCT lead to empirical tests. The statutes of rational choice do not rest on readily identifiable sets of empirical success. Political scientists and sociologists alike have noted that only rarely has it led to "rigorous empirical analysis of real world . . . behavior" (see McKelvey and Rosenthal 1978:405-406). Most journals and book-length anthologies in the social and political sciences have not addressed the empirical successes of rational choice models (for a more complete list, see Green and Shapiro 1994[2]).

In sum, although RCT purports to generate universal theories of social, political, and economic behavior, the fact that it ignores empirical tests and explains phenomena in an ad hoc manner undermines its claims. Furthermore, its application to particular, individual behavior such as purchase selection and voting further attests to its lack of generalizability to collective social action. Rather, RCT deals with such individual decisions as the "logic of free-riding" (Olson [1965] 1971:16) and the logic of why it is irrational to vote, whereas Green and Shapiro (1994) focus on the major literature from RCT, which has been subjected to close, serious, empirical scrutiny and has survived. Green and Shapiro (1994) allege that rational choice hypotheses tend to support "propositions that are banal. Furthermore, rational choice hypotheses are too often formulated in ways that are inherently resistant to genuine empirical testing, raising serious questions about whether rational choice scholarship can properly be regarded as social science" (p. 9).

To this author and to organizational analysis, which is an applied science, this is a (the) critical limitation of RCT.

Conclusion

For rational choice theorists, individual rationality is largely a matter of choices based on preferences. Difficulties presented by the need for choices to be consistent, complete, and transitive are overcome by invoking revealed preferences theory, which states that choices are rational because they are based on preferences that are known through the choices that are made. Collective rationality is not defined as any kind of action taken by a group as a whole, but as individual actions aggregated to produce an outcome that somehow benefits everyone. An action is irrational only if it is inconsistent, incomplete, or intransitive. Rational actions must demonstrate causal connections and are based on the principle of maximizing utility, and no references to the substance of the choice are needed for it to be rational.

Although utility theory, upon which RCT is built, is normative in that it posits what choices should be, namely rational, it does not concern itself with the substance of choices. It does not matter that the goals of actors might be dangerous or that the qualities possessed by actors might be evil. As long as choices fit within the guidelines of consistency, completeness and transitivity, they are rational. Here, context is irrelevant. The rational actor is not exactly the same as the economic actor. The former need only exhibit consistent preferences that lead to consistent actions, whereas the latter must be not only consistent but complete, continuous, and, of course, selfish.

There are many problems in applying RCT to organizations, not the least of which is the fact that RCT works well only in an ideal, theoretical, model-building context, whereas the organizations it attempts to analyze are dynamic, real-world entities that exist in a constant state of flux. Because the quality of context independence in RCT is implicit rather than openly stated, the problems for organizational theorists using this theory are magnified because real-world choices made in and by organizations are always context dependent.

Notes

1. Unicity asks the question, "Is there *one* rational course of action?" (Rawls 1971). Unicity is distinguished "optimality" (Is the rational course the *best* course?)

2. For example, see the October 1992 issue of *Rationality & Society*, edited by James Coleman; James Coleman and Thomas Fararo's *Rational Choice Theory: Advocacy and Critique* (1993); Jon Elster's anthology, titled *Rational Choice* (1986); and Kristen Monroe's *Economic Approach to Politics* (1991b). Although they analyze empirical issues, they do not analyze the empirical success of RCT in explaining social phenomena. The empirical power of the theory is yet to be assessed.

CHAPTER 3

Basic Characteristics of Rational Choice Models versus Organizational Theories

Assumptions

Charles Schultze, former president of the American Economic Association, stated, "The one great thing we have going for us is the premise that individuals act rationally in trying to satisfy their preferences. That is an incredibly powerful tool, because you can model it" (quoted in Kuttner 1985:75)

Whereas organizational theory turns to economic and rational choice models, RCT seems to be experiencing its own crisis. In particular, the primary assumption of rationality is being questioned within economics itself. Rational choice's modeling of human behavior, deduced from the core assumption that humans act rationally, is elegant and consistent. Recently, it has made increasing claims of universal applicability to all kinds of entities and units of analysis, from the economic and social to the individual, group, and organization, but it does not describe the actual experience of real people.

Rational choice theorists agree that certain requirements must be part of the definition of rationality. Two of these requirements are consistency and transitivity. Consistency demands that it must be possible for all of the decision maker's options to be rank ordered. The assumption of consistency is also called the assumption of connectedness. Each preference must be either equal or unequal. Unequal preferences can be rank ordered for comparison across the decision maker's entire set of preferences. RCT does not require that numerical values be attached to preferences or that comparison be made across decision makers. It only assumes the possibility of rank-ordered preferences.

Rational choice theorists also assume "that preference orderings are transitive. If A is preferred to B, and B is preferred to C, then consistency requires that A is preferred to C" (Green and Shapiro 1994:14-5). The amount of preference of one choice over another is not specified by RCT. The distance between preferences or magnitude of preferences does not have to be known to those holding those preferences or to the analyst. Kenneth Arrow (1951:1-3) and others describe this as "a weak ordering of preference."

Another assumption made by rational choice theorists is that individuals "maximize the expected value of their payoff measured on some utility scale" and that, usually, "numerical probabilities can be attached to different eventualities" (Luce and Raiffa 1957:50). Eventuality is calculated as the value of the outcome "weighted by the probability of achieving it" (Elster 1986; Harsanyi 1986).

Rational choice theorists assume that their models apply equally to all people under analysis—decision-making rules and preferences are stable across individuals and time. Allowing for assumptions of interpersonal variation produces enormous tractability problems (Strom 1990:126). Altruistic behavior is discounted by RCT, because any model that would explain such behavior would be required to include some variety in human motivation. The only motive allowed by rational choice assumption is self-interest (Goetze and Galderisi

1989:38). The quality of parsimony is used to justify eliminating all variation in motivation. If the behavior of some organizational members must be explained by one model and other behavior by another model, because some are male and others are female, or because some are managers and others are workers, or some are owners and others are not, then a single parsimonious model may not mirror the empirical world. In all organizations, two or more models must be used to explain unparsimonious actions scientifically.

In sum, the instrumental conception of individual rationality of maximizing behavior to achieve expected utility does not correspond to organizational empirical meanings and resulting action. Rationality is seldom monogenous across individuals.

Table 3.1 contrasts the fundamentally different intellectual premises, characteristics, and methodologies of rational choice and organizational theories. Organizational analysis is not a unified field: it has a variety of perspectives, both mainstream and peripheral. Rational choice and organizational analyses differ in their theoretical assumptions, their concepts and theory, their methodology, and their implications.

Intellectual Heritage

As a subdiscipline, neoclassical economic theory, out of which the rational choice model of organizations developed, precedes the development of organizational theory. European organizational theory has its roots in the writings of Max Weber (1947), and U.S. organizational theory has its roots in the thought of early scientific and classical management theory. The debate between these two schools of thought has taken on real meaning in the 1990s, as is demonstrated in the debate between Jay B. Barney (1990) and Lex Donaldson (1990a and 1990b) in the *Academy of Management Review*.

The exponents of RCT argue that it is the queen science on which all other social sciences are based, and that it will inevitably and

Table 3.1   Rational Choice Theory and Organizational Theory:
Ideal Type Contrasts

	RCT	OT
Assumptions about human nature	Rational	Rational Emotional Habitual Normative
	Greedy and self-interested Maximizer Instrumental	Self- and other-interested Variable levels acceptable Instrumental and reflexive, expressive
	Fixed hierarchy of preferences	Fluid preferences
Unit of analysis	Individual	Collective (organizational or interorganizational)
Concepts of organization	Nominal Aggregate of individuals	Real Sui generis and beyond the individual
Philosophical stances	Hobbesian Exchange	Platonic Behaviorist, interpretive, explanatory
Power	Does not question origin or position	Power, that which provides access to position
Modes of theorizing	Deductive	Inductive Axiomatic Data-driven
Methods	Model testing Quantitative, but not empirical	Theory constructing and hypothesis testing Empirical quantitative, and qualitative data
Criteria for validity	Ideal Predictive	Realistic Explanatory
Controls	Market Markets control corporations	Environment, other orga- nizations, uncertainty Corporations create markets

ultimately incorporate the analysis of all social behavior. This position is exemplified by Hirschleifer's (1986) statement:

> As economics imperialistically employs its tools of analysis over a wide range of social issues, it will become sociology and anthropology and political science. But correspondingly, as these other disciplines grow increasingly rigorous, they will not merely resemble, but will be economics. It is in this sense that "economics" is taken here as broadly synonymous with social science. (pp. 321-22)

As is demonstrated by the work of Oliver Williamson (1975), Barney and William G. Ouchi (1986), and Michael Jensen (1983), some economic organizational analysts and some management theorists have moved uncritically in this direction. Only recently have others begun to question the seemingly total acceptance of such assumptions in transaction cost and agency perspectives (for exceptions, see Donaldson 1990a, 1990b).

Philosophical Stance

Both RCT and contemporary organizational theory rest on ideas about the nature of man and of social organizations that originated in the 17th and 18th centuries. The two major thinkers who contributed most to modern theory are Thomas Hobbes (1588-1679), a monarchist who fled to the European continent during the English Civil War, and Jean Jacques Rousseau (1712-1778), a French philosopher who was abandoned at the age of 10 by his widowed father. After spending many years as a vagabond, he gained the fame and wealth he craved by winning a contest sponsored by the Academy of Dijon with an essay, "Discourse on the Sciences and the Arts," in which he accused society of corrupting humanity.

The personal experiences of these two men led them to their respective, and quite opposite, views of human nature. For Hobbes, people are naturally mean, selfish, and violent, whereas Rousseau sees men as peaceful and one with the environment when allowed to live in a state of nature—it is society that brings problems to humans. Economic theorists, including those who use RCT, adopt a more Hobbesian view when they characterize all human motivation as only self-serving, selfish, and maximizing. Organizational theorists, on the other hand, think in more complex terms and accept many types of motivation for human behavior.

Hobbes's most recognized work, *Leviathan* ([1651] 1968), depicts the "state of nature" as the "war of each against all" and defines power as a precondition of social order and peace (p. 150). Power is man's "present means to obtain some future apparent good" (p. 150). "Man" spends his whole life seeking and acquiring more and more power in order to have a good life. In addition to the need for power, another natural condition of man is "equality." People are equal to one another in their physical and especially their mental capacities. Because even physically weaker individuals can prevail by using their wits, everyone has an equal hope of succeeding in the world.

However, the natural state of man is not at all a pleasant one. Because everyone can hope for the same gain, unless resources are without limit, conflict is inevitable. Hobbes ([1651] 1968) writes, "If any two men desire the same thing, which nevertheless they cannot both enjoy, they become enemies; and in the way of their End, . . . endeavor to destroy or subdue one another" (p. 16). Thus, war is not only the natural product of man's will to power and his equality of hope of securing his needs, but also an expression of his contentious nature. War is not simply actual combat but a condition of human life. "The consequences of such a war are that men live without culture and without society" (Zeitlin 1997:20). For Hobbes, the life of men is "solitary, poore, nasty, brutish and short" (Hobbes [1651] 1968:186). Because man exists in a state of nature without benefit of society—with its concern for justice and ethical behavior—his life is fraught with violence and deception.

Because natural man is such a self-interested savage, how is society possible at all? According to Hobbes ([1651] 1968), it is the "common power to feare" (p. 223) that impels men to join together to impose order on the human condition. No one can survive in a world where everyone is always at war with everyone else, so a glimmer of reason surfaces to guide men toward devising a way to control their natural instincts. The result is the social contract. Men agree to relinquish the freedom they enjoyed in their natural state in exchange for protection from the unbridled competition and violence inflicted by a "war of each against all" (p. 223).

Of course, the sovereign authority responsible for protecting the newborn Society must enforce the contract with the threat of violence, because the peace and stability it brings is jeopardized constantly by the individual's need for power. It is only because men turn over all their power to the Sovereign that Society (the Commonwealth) can come into being. Hobbes ([1651] 1968) characterizes the Commonwealth as "the great Leviathan" and likens it to a "*Mortal God*, to which we owe under the *Immortal God*, our peace and defense" (p. 227). It is clear that for Hobbes, human beings can achieve peace only within the Society created by the social contract, because without it, we are naturally warlike and deceptive.

This position is not unlike that of Oliver Williamson (1975), who defines man in social organizations (specifically, markets) as opportunistic, "self-interest seeking with guile" (p. 9), meaning that man is calculatively selfish by nature and under conditions of scarce resources moves from market structures to hierarchies (corporations) in order to increase returns and therefore maximize his security.

In contrast, for Rousseau, natural man is perfectible, and social systems should be judged by the degree to which they facilitate his perfection. He conceived the ideal state of nature to be the perfect balance between humanity's needs and its basic resources. This relationship was of equilibrium and was upset only by a corrupt society. Rousseau offered his criticisms of society in a variety of works, but it is in *The Social Contract and Discourses* (1762), a classic of political science, that he develops his ideas about society and government.

Rousseau argues that to assume that men made society and submitted to a strong central power to escape the war of nature is wrong. Men make war only as a result of social inequality that arises within and between classes. Social conditions in which some are rich and some poor, in which some dominate and some serve, give rise to hostility and conflict. For Rousseau, the causal chain is that social conditions lead to inequality, inequality leads to war, and war leads to the formation of social contracts (organizations) and especially the state. Thus, Rousseau argued that government originated to protect the property of the wealthy. Obligation and property rights were a product of society.

Thus, social contracts are coercive, absurd, and unreasonable, and instead of inwardly uniting individual wills, members are compelled to unite in unstable relationships that are devoid of ethical foundations. Williamson (1975) and Jensen and Meckling's (1976) concepts of modern capitalism stand in sharp contrast to Rousseau's ideas of the perfectibility of man. Because those who own and control capital are sovereign over those who serve the corporation (both workers and clients), the social inequality between those with inequal property is unavoidable.

Coleman (1990:421-50, 531-664) makes assumptions that are consistent with the Hobbesian argument (Hobbes [1651] 1966) when he holds that corporations grow inasmuch as it is more beneficial for individual actors in large systems to delegate rights to some acting bodies than to retain such rights for themselves. Coleman does not take into account that corporations can be established and expanded by powerful actors simply by using their power regardless of benefits to other actors. Rights do not have to be delegated by power holders.

Assumptions about the Nature of Humans

One of the most basic differences between rational choice and most organizational theories lies in their assumptions about the nature of humans. Humans, or "man," of neoclassical economic theory and its rational choice derivatives are selfish and greedy, or at least exclusively self-interested. These characteristics are tied to the Hobbesian view of the human condition. The famous *homo economicus* is rational, self-interested, instrumental, and optimizing, and he has a fixed set of preferences. On the other hand, the human beings of organizational theories vary from tabula rasa to constrained and generally are defined as of less import than collectivities, but also as more complex. They are variably motivated by rationality; emotions (Flam 1988, 1990); socialization (Fligstein 1990a, 1990b; Meyer and Rowan 1977); habit (Camic 1986); and social relationships (Granovetter 1985; Zey 1992), or some mixture of any or all of these (Etzioni 1986; Katz 1988; Mansbridge 1990a, 1990b).

Whereas humans are purely instrumental in their behavior according to RCT, they are expressive, self-reflective, and uncertain in organizational theories. Strictly materialistic behavior is not the sole force motivating human behavior for organizational theorists. These more complex humans interact with, change, and are constrained by the organizations that they create.

The central fallacy of RCT is that it postulates a single motivation, self-interest, as an explanation for all human behavior, economic and otherwise. The second fallacy is that the meaning of "rationality," here self-interest, is limited to the orientation of action toward maximum conformity to a norm (an institutionalized motivation that is learned in the course of social experiences). Organizational theorists might well assume that strictly materialistic behavior is learned in the same way as other behavior and is not the sole force motivating all human behavior. Organizations are not derived de novo in each interaction from individual choices; rather, individual choice presumes the prior existence of society for organizational theorists, and it previews choices. Organizational theorists see whatever motivations are in place as socially learned and changing, not atomistically and permanently chosen. Social action is understood not only by looking at the economics of the situation but also by looking at institutional structures, goals, social norms, and cultural values.

Mode of Theorizing

Rational choice theorists deduce axioms from their assumptions, whereas organizational theorists, making fewer assumptions to begin with, investigate empirically the nature of organizations and their relationships with other organizations. Rational choice theorists do not need to ground their research because they assume the grounding; then, they use highly abstracted secondary data to develop elegant, parsimonious models to predict (in fact, they often use the term "explain") human behavior.

Many organizational theorists take rational choice assumptions themselves to be problematic. In each study, the rationality of individual decision making, Weber's rationality of organizations, and the orientation of individuals as a historical process in the development of organizations, respectively, have been major subjects of organizational theory and research.

The truth value of organizational theory depends not on the logical connection of a set of predefined assumptions but on empirical support for theories. In contrast, rational choice theorists do not question whether their assumptions fit reality in different historical, cultural, or institutional circumstances. They define essential aspects of the development of organizations as external to RCT models and deliberately avoid questions crucial to understanding organizations. RCT seeks to derive "universally applicable hypotheses . . . which transcend [specific] institutional, systematic, and historical variation" (Wilber and Jameson 1983:32). Such variation is "noise" or "white noise" (Williamson 1975) to be disregarded or excluded by moving to another level of analysis, usually one more micro in nature. To the extent that organizational theorists accept RCT, they, too, will be unable to analyze historical, cultural, and institutional variations and changes. When rational choice theorists analyze empirical data, they often select historical periods that most approximate the assumptions of their ideal model.

Rational choice theorists extrapolate from assumptions to predict social action of individuals. Although organizational theorists

.are interested in predictive models, they are more interested in explaining why organizations act as they do. Organizational theorists seek to be realistic in explaining what exists and how it changes, whereas rational choice theorists seek to predict what will happen given a set of ideal circumstances, if all else is held constant. Explaining why is not part of the model. The explanation is taken as given, and being right about the prediction for the wrong reasons is of no consequence to rational choice theorists. However, for organizational theorists, the wrong reason is as incorrect as the wrong model.

Methodology

A study conducted by Nobel Prize-winning economist Wassily Leontief (Kuttner 1985:78), in which he analyzed the articles in *The American Economic Review* from 1977 to 1981, found that 54 percent of the articles used mathematical models without data; only one half of 1 percent of the articles were empirical analyses of original data generated by the articles' authors. When data are used to test economic models, they are usually ignored, trivialized, or made the exception when they run counter to the assumptions of the model. Rather, games are created in which the data mirror the model so as to meet false assumptions and contradict empirical data. Support and retention of the model are more important to RCT than whether the model mirrors the data. The tendency to search for data sets that support the model is more likely than the alternative, that the researcher will alter the model to fit empirical reality. In contrast, psychologists and organizational psychologists are more likely to test and alter the assumptions of the rational choice model when the data do not support the model (Tversky and Kahneman 1974, 1981).

Critics of RCT point out that the assumptions of rationality can be restated as psychologically subjective self-interest, and because of this, propositions derived from them are irrefutable. They simply explain that whatever the choice of behavior, the actor was maximizing. When the behavior is masochistic, such as committing suicide or staying in a relationship in which he or she is continually beaten, the behavior is explained as being less costly than leaving a child or the shame the person would bear if he or she had not made that choice. There are several problems here. First, this model does not leave room for behavior *that is not based* on choice, that is, coerced behavior. Second, because all behavior is seen as an exchange of costs and benefits, it is assumed that the individual maximizes in each transaction. In fact, an individual may be beaten to within an inch of her life, but this is neither a fair exchange, maximization, nor an act of choice on the part of the subject. All of these are assumptions of RCT that completely disregard the nature of many power relationships. The inability to analyze or explain power is a critical problem of RCT.

Rational choice theorists often use data that are grossly aggregated across organizational types to create large samples. Organizational theorists have been explicit about the limitation of aggregating across organizational types. For example, the Aston group found different results when controlling industrial, production, and service organizations.[1] Effects washed out when these three types of organizations were aggregated. Likewise, Peter Blau and Richard A. Schoenherr (1971) alert organizational analysts to their concern about generalizing across organizational types, much less aggregating data across types.

Yet another empirically related problem with economic analysis of large aggregated samples is that although the variances explained are small, the relationship is statistically significant because of the large sample size created by gross aggregation. Organizational studies that control for type of organization and that rest on smaller sample sizes result in larger explained variances because the relationships actually exist in the data rather than resulting from the large sample size. Data that are aggregated across organization type result in statistically significant findings that describe relationships inaccurately or describe weak relationships that appear to be statistically significant only because of inflated sample size. However, these relationships mirror more elegant models that are more publishable than are less elegant models that are empirically based.

Comparison of Organizational and Rational Choice Theories

Organizational theorists separate out more dimensions of complex realities, whereas rational choice theorists restrict themselves to one way of approaching problems. For example, let us look at the studies of corporate directors and at theories of agency, ownership, and control, all concerns of both types of theories. Even when there is convergence between what is studied by each, the conclusions are widely divergent because the questions asked by each discipline are of little interest to the other and based on entirely different assumptions. Rational choice theorists take the market as an unchallengeable independent force beyond the control of individual investors and corporate actors, whereas organizational theorists see the market as made up of organizational exchanges much like any other exchanges between organizations—which are manipulated by corporations, investment bankers, and commercial bankers (Mintz and Schwartz 1984, 1985; Zey 1993). RCT agency theorists have generalized RCT to encompass questions about organizations and managers, whereas organizational theory has extended the study of organizations to include the analysis of markets, as well as substantive topics such as managerial incentives, the transformation of corporate control, and transfer pricing. Although both perspectives examine the same substantive questions about organizations, because of differing assumptions, they produce vastly different findings.

Agency theory has more recently become the dominant hegemonic paradigm underlying most corporate governance research, however, psychologists and sociologists have long suggested theoretical limits of agency theory (for examples, see Hirsch et al.

1987; Perrow 1986; and work cited in Zey 1992). The basic link of agency theory to organizational theory is that according to agency theory, losses to the principal (shareholders) resulting from interest divergences between managers and their agents may be curbed by imposing control/governance structures upon the agent. These governance structures are primarily economic disincentives to move the agent's interest into alignment with the principals.

The pivotal point of the limitations of agency theory result from assumptions about individual utility motivations resulting in divergent interests of principals and agents. Exclusive reliance on neoclassical, economic-based agency theory is undesirable in explaining organizational behavior because of the complexities of organizations. Like Doucouliagos (1994), I hold that additional and sometimes contradictory assumptions are needed to explain organizational relationships between various actions in organizations.

The relationship between stockholders and managers of a firm is the pure agent/principal relationship because it is based on the separation of ownership and control (Berle and Means 1932; Jensen and Meckling 1976). At the center of agency theory are assumptions about the nature of humans that are based in two centuries of neoclassical economic premises and theorizing. The model of humans in agency theory is that of rational actors who seek to maximize individual utility (Jensen and Meckling 1976). Through free choice, both agents and principals as social actors seek to gain as much utility as possible with the least possible expenditure.

The separation of ownership of property from the management of that property in large, complex corporations separated ownership control from management control. Berle and Means (1932) theorize that because of the large capital base required to meet a firm's economic obligations and the large number of managers needed to control the work process of large multinational corporations, owners are unable to secure the maximum gain for themselves because it is humanly impossible to manage such a corporation alone. Therefore, the large number of shareholders (owners) contract with managers who are legally responsible. Reciprocally, managers contract with owners (principals) to maximize their own personal gain. However, principals must protect their interests against that of maximizing, utility-seeking managers through governance systems. If the utility functions of self-interested agents and principals are aligned, there is no agency problem because both parties benefit from an increase in individual utility. However, if they are not aligned, it is only principals who bear the agency costs associated with divergent interests of agents and principals. In fact, cost may also be incurred by managers. In corporations, the situation in which agents do not share the same interests and utility choices as their principals is substantial.

Agency theory assumes that in uncertain situations in which principals do not know which agents are most opportunistic, the principals limit potential losses to the interest of their agents through governance mechanisms (Williamson 1985). The purpose (goal) of agency theory is to reduce the agency costs incurred by principals by imposing internal controls to eliminate an agent's self-serving behavior (Jensen and Meckling 1976). If the agent insists on maximizing his or her self-interested behavior, more costly, external control tactics (such as acquisitions, mergers, divestures) become necessary (Walsh and Seward 1990). It may seem more necessary to privatize the fees if control cannot be realized in any other manner. Because external mechanisms are so expensive, principals prefer to use internal methods to maximize utility (Walsh and Seward 1990).

To lower costs for agents and to protect shareholders' interests, a variety of control strategies are suggested by agency theorists. Organizational analysis has focused on two such control mechanisms: (1) compensation schemes for agents and (2) governance structures. Financial incentive programs offer benefits that are expected to align the interests of agents with the more powerful interests of principals (shareholders) as rewards for meeting shareholder objectives (rewards to managers are tied to return to shareholders). Such programs are effective controls in corporations when the agent has substantial power based on knowledge and information and the policing of agents by principals is difficult or simply not feasible.

Governance structures that are focused on making agents' behavior compatible with their principals' interest include audits and performance evaluations of managers (see Edwards 1979). Control of board members, who are the official communicators of shareholders' objectives and interest to managers and monitor managers' response, is a more difficult and less direct method of controlling agents/managers.

Principal control of agents is central to agency theory because agency theorists hold that the interests of agents and those of principals always diverge because they assume that at every opportunity the agent will maximize his or her individual benefits or rewards at the expense of the principal's benefit. This is the point at which RCT can be integrated into the model of agency theory. Both assume that humans are inherently opportunistic (Williamson 1975). It follows that, to the degree that controls are imperfect, opportunism is ever present in organizations. The delegation of authority to managers by owners permits agents/managers to opportunistically promote their own self-interest at the expense of that of the principals. Principals are assumed to delegate authority to managers and control the actions of managers if managers abuse this authority (Jensen and Meckling 1976).

The assumption that humans are "self-serving and self-interested" has been criticized by both those who advocate agency theory and those who write against it. The former, represented by Jensen and Meckling (1994), find this model of humans to be oversimplified and unrealistic, appropriate only for mathematical models. Doucouliagos (1994) agreed that human motivation is often more complex than simple self-interest, and Frank (1994) further inferred that this way of characterizing humans is not adequate to explain real life. However, Hirsch et al. (1987) made the most insightful criticism for our analysis when they noted that the trade-off between elegance and realism in this model results in a serious reduction in the generalizability of agency theory.

The critical limitation of agency theory is that in situations of zero sum games, it cannot explain relationships where parties are at odds in conflict and their behavior cannot be reconciled through monitoring and compensation systems (i.e., where the managers' power is based on power other than authority and cannot be controlled by control of wealth-based authority).

For example, William Domhoff (1970, 1974, 1978, 1979, 1983, 1987, 1990) views corporations as hegemonies controlled by both inside and outside directors who garner their power from their social class. Maurice Zeitlin (1974, 1980) also views the control of corporations as originating outside of corporations in social classes, but here, control is lodged in those who hold wealth as a part of old, established families that have intermarried with other wealthy families. They control corporations though ownership. Organizational theorists such as Jeffrey Pfeffer (1992) and David Gordon (1980) take a more middle-of-the-road approach, seeing inside directors and top management as dominant coalitions in the control of corporations, whereas outside directors are of less consequence. Bank control theorists, including Mintz and Schwartz (1984, 1985), see many corporations as more dependent on some resources than on others (i.e., capital), and this dependency places the control of corporations completely outside of both the inside and outside directors and corporate management, and into the hands of bankers. Banks are, of course, simply another type of corporation, and who controls commercial banks and investment banks is another question.

The rational choice perspective views the corporation as a "corporate actor" (Coleman 1990; Jensen 1983, 1986, 1988, 1989a, 1989b) in which control is taken out of the hands of both inside and outside directors and top management. Corporations are viewed as controlled by the discipline of the marketplace, and corporate managers and boards of directors are merely epiphenomenal agents of market forces. In Coleman's (1990) case, the market involved is that of exchange between individuals. In Jensen's case, it is the market in corporation control that is played out in the mergers and acquisitions of the 1980s. This same view is congruent with the population ecology of organizations; that is, functional organizations are merely selected out (rewarded) by the (all-knowing) "environment." Social entities, management groups, and boards of directors have little, if any, power to exert. They make choices, but the choices do not have positive major consequences unless they make the organization conform better to market mechanisms.

The idea that corporations are controlled by the discipline of the marketplace hardly presents a complete or accurate picture of reality. It represents an idealized image of market (or environmental) forces that is questionable at best. Indeed, in an earlier time, the idealized reality of the large corporations and their owners/directors was seen as the force that drove the marketplace (see Chandler 1962, 1977, 1990a, 1990b). Organizational theory is more attentive to multiple explanations than are rational choice/market models; therefore, it offers a more complete and accurate model of corporate control over time than the choice model. Organizational theory is more observant of the variety of conditions in the real world, and although neoclassical economic theory and its extension to RCT presents the simpler and more unified model, it can only be relied upon to always predict the same results. In contrast, organizational theory relies on empirical evidence and is thus more accurate in describing relationships that actually take place. There is no advantage in predicting what only happens in an idealized model.

Macro-Micro Links

As was noted earlier in this chapter, rational choice theorists make Hobbesian arguments in explaining control. The same is true in explaining control in and of large organizations (see Coleman 1990:421-50, 531-663). The argument is that individuals who own organizations, such as principals, make sure that corporations do not act against their interest when they increase benefits but raise costs. Accordingly, they argue that what is needed is the revitalization of small units by decentralization and control of corporate actors through incentives. There is only a small leap to management ownership as the major benefit. The merging of management and ownership avoids the principal/agent problem and eliminates competing interests in controlling organizations. Again, this is an Hobbesian argument that does not take into account that powerful corporations can be established and expanded by powerful actors simply by using their power regardless of the benefits to other actors.

Further decentralization has its negative effects as well as positive. It sharpens the inequality between the departments and divisions in the decentralized organization. The inequalities between rich and poor departments, divisions, and subsidiaries, between powerful and less powerful units, and between growing and declining units will be strengthened. We can see this by taking a quick glance at the decentralized system created at Drexel Burnham Lambert, where the High Yield Bond Department was able to use its relative economic power not only to exploit other departments but to control the corporation (Zey 1993).

Enormous, multidivisional, global corporations that are increasingly more complex than most national states cannot be governed through decentralization of formal rules and regulations and individualization of reward structures as is advocated by agency theory (Jensen 1983, 1986, 1988, 1989a, 1989b). Decentralized, economically liberal corporations in which everyone looks after only his or her own self-interest often self-destruct. There must be other characteristics of contemporary, multidivisional, global corporations that reach beyond the identification of modern society with liberal society in the narrow sense of the coordinated liberty of economically self-interested individuals to explain their functioning.

There are many ways to make macro-micro links between individual action and organizational action or organizational networks, including through causal relationships or through demonstrating meanings (cultural links). For example, Coleman (1990:1-23) redirects and supplies a new meaning for Weber's ([1920-21a] 1972a, [1920-21b] 1972b, [1920-21c] 1971) classical explanation of the rise of the capitalist spirit because of the emergence of the Protestant ethic in the Western world (see Munch, 1992a, chap. 7 for a more complete explanation). In keeping with his rational choice perspective and his use of economic predictive models, Coleman explains the relationship between these two otherwise macro-level phenomena as a macro-micro relationship. He holds that in the context of the Protestant community,

> it was more beneficial for the capitalist to accumulate wealth through hard work and reliable behavior without becoming addicted to the vices of a luxurious life-style because such behavior was rewarded by the members of that community with social approval and the acknowledgement that one belonged to God's "Elect," where any deviation from that path was punished by disapproval and by being grouped among the eternally condemned. (Munch 1992a:156-57)

Although this economic calculation may have played a part in the minds of some, Munch holds that economic calculations played a minor role and that what was more important and occasioned deeper analysis on the part of Weber was that a consistent relationship indeed existed between the meaning of the Protestant ethic and the meaning of the spirit of capitalism (Munch 1992a:157). The proof of the adequacy of meaning in his explanation (in contrast to the adequacy of cause that posits the overrepresentation of Protestants among entrepreneurs and professionals and the rise of modern rational capitalism in Protestant geographic areas) was Weber's overwhelming focus not only in the study of the development of capitalism but throughout his comparative works. Munch goes on to point out that the greater part of Weber's explanation involves efforts to reconstruct cultural meaning-relationships, "a task for which RCT has no sensitivity at all because it does not seem to exist for rational choice theorists. Culture cannot be reduced to a variable in a deductive-nomological explanation" (Munch 1992a:159). According to Munch (1992a, 1992b), further interpretive explanations rather than causal predictions are needed.

For rational choice theorists, the objective is to explain micro individual human behavior as a result of macro conditions as they are taken into account in the preferences of rational actors in their choice of the most beneficial way to act. Such an explanation excludes the various meaning-relationships that are the bases of action and fails to address the fact that actors make decisions to act on a number of complex bases, including group loyalty, trust, cooperation, legitimacy, and authority.

Conclusion

The differences between RCT and organizational theory encompass all possible dimensions, with the exception that theorists from both perspectives often look at the same aspects of society. However, the conclusions of each differ widely, because not only are the underlying philosophy and assumptions about human nature quite disparate, but the theoretical process and methods themselves are fundamentally dissimilar for each. Whereas RCT restricts its view of human motivation to self-interest in all cases, organizational theory allows a fuller range of motives for human action. As a consequence, organizational theory must be empirical and data driven in order to get a true look at human activity. In contrast, rational choice theorists construct beautiful, predictive models and tend to overlook data that do not fit. Although it is tempting for some organizational theorists to turn to the principles of RCT, only economic issues can be analyzed by doing so. Because organizations and society itself are built on relationships, it is important for any effective social theory to be able to address them adequately. RCT cannot sufficiently explain most social relationships.

Note

1. The Aston group studies were dominant in the 1960s and 1970s. For example, see Pugh et al.'s "Dimensions of Organization Structure" (1968); John Child's "Organization Structure and Strategies of Control: A Replication of the Aston Studies" (1972); Johannes Pennings' "Measure of Organizational Structure: A Methodological Note" (1973:688); and Peter M. Blau's "The Comparative Study of Organizations" (1965:323).

CHAPTER 4

Critique of Rational
Choice Theory's Explanations
of Social Relationships

The Nature of Power

According to rational choice theory (RCT), *power* is itself a result of economic calculations and transactions (Coleman 1990). In turn, unequal power is a structural condition that results in unequal benefits in interaction. That is, the greater one person's power over another, the greater will be the gap between his or her benefits and those of the other. This relationship will continue to exist as long as both parties are better off in the relationship than if they exited or revolted. According to Coleman (1990:489-99), revolution is rare because most of the time, the subordinate does not expect greater benefits from revolution than from maintenance of the relationship.

RCT does not explain the origins of the unequal relationship. If, in the beginning, everyone was equal and acted rationally, how did some benefit more than others from interactions? Is unequal power a result of unequal distribution of resources resulting from exploitation of some by others because of patriarchal relationships that have been passed down through history, or are they a result of the unequal distribution of authority within organizations? RCT does not explain how unequal distribution of power began.

The proposition for rational choice theorists is that subordinates stay in relationships as long as they do not expect greater benefits from withdrawal from or revolution against the superordinate. This proposition makes several possibly erroneous assumptions. First, that the subordinate is in the power relationship by choice, and second, that the subordinate has the power to choose to exit the relationship. In a democracy, we are more likely to assume that economic choices are voluntary and that relationships are also voluntary. However, this is by no means the nature of power relationships (e.g., for slaves, inmates of prisons and asylums, abused spouses, and employees), because in such relationships, the subordinate is subjected to the wishes of the superordinate. The subordinate is forced to refrain from or to carry out action that he or she, under conditions of free choice, would not perform. Those without power can be subjected to pressure to continue a relationship that results in nothing but costs and no benefits, even when any other alternative would provide greater benefits and fewer costs. Those who cannot get another job, cannot leave prison, or cannot escape an abusive relationship have no alternatives available to them. If the subordinate attempts to withdraw from the relationship, he or she cannot because the superordinate forces him or her to stay; or external conditions in the environment limit exit; or an internal psychological state of the subordinate, such as fear, constrains his or her action. The subordinate may be physically restrained, or the superordinate may have the ability to shape the subordinate's objective situation or subjective perception of the situation to such an extent that the subordinate or someone he or she loves will be injured as a result of any attempt to leave or revolt. These costs may be real, or they may *appear* to be real. Regardless, they have the same effect.

The source of power over others may be the possession of expertise or knowledge that shapes the other party's perception of the situation or limits access to exit, outside relationships, or individual or collective goods. Rational choice theorists do not analyze the sources or bases of power. They deal with the immediate interaction episode and attempt to explain it through economic transactions, that is, that any alternative way of acting would be even more costly. Because they look only for economic explanations, they cannot see the bases of power. It is the economics of the subordinate that is under scrutiny, and this, and only this, is explainable by RCT. The task of the rational choice theorist, then, is to explain why the party that continually bears the greatest costs in the relationship will incur even greater costs if he or she withdraws from the relationship (not being able to find another job, not being able to support oneself or one's family, shame, imprisonment, or death). This task is facilitated by assuming that each interaction is a separate and different transaction in which free choices are made. However, it is the very fact that they are not free that further deepens the relationship and secures the bonds of power.

If the relationship is seen as social, with the multiple bases of power that exist in social relationships, one can explain *why* the subordinate is in a situation in which he or she has no better alternative than continuing with an action that only enhances his or her net costs. The superordinate may have the power of physical coercion, resources the subordinate needs, exclusive ability to eliminate affective bonds, or superior knowledge. *The explanation of cause is at the heart of a social theory of power and cannot be reduced to the economic exchanges of rational choice theory.* Because RCT cannot explain the continuation of such relationships, it has only limited explanatory power and cannot serve as the exclusive core of a truly comprehensive theory of organizations.

Potential versus Actual Power

From the rational choice perspective, the superordinate also benefits more from staying within the relationship than from any other alternative. Whether this party will make use of its power and to what extent it will do so depends again, without exception, on the utility calculation of benefits, preferences, and expectations of success. However, precisely because the transaction is part of a continual, ongoing relationship, there is a point at which the threat of application of power becomes more costly for the superordinate. Because the rational calculation of separate costs and benefits is based on selfish interests and cannot take into account the perspective of the other, the superordinate cannot know about the costs to the subordinate. In addition, the superordinate cannot know that he or she is undermining the trust, motivation, cooperation, loyalty, and commitment of the subordinate.

In some relationships, the superordinate depends more heavily on the trust, motivation, cooperation, loyalty, and commitment of the subordinate than in other relationships. These relationships are also found in complex organizations and associations and in other relationships in which the power differential between the subordinate and the superordinate is not as great as those previously discussed. That is, these relationships are more voluntary and more market-like—the kind of relationships that rational choice purports to explain best. The more the superordinate depends on trust, motivation, cooperation, loyalty, and commitment, the less it can use or threaten to use various sources of power that reduce trust, motivation, cooperation, loyalty, and commitment. In this situation, even if the subordinate cannot revolt or leave the relationship, at least he or she can comply with little motivation and cooperation, leaving the superordinate worse off than if the subordinate could have complied with trust, motivation, cooperation, loyalty, and commitment.

Herein lies the importance of the explanation of *why* the subordinate stays in the relationship, which is beyond the economics of the power relationship. The subordinate may have no alternative outside the relationship, but he or she may have alternatives within the relationship, and choosing to stay in the relationship may actually reduce the utility outcomes of the superordinate. The more the subordinate can affect the outcomes of the superordinate, the more he or she has power over the superordinate. If the subordinate gradually gains more power with each successive interaction, the power relationship becomes more equal. Equal power based in a given source such as family ties may be impossible; however, the balance of power over all sources may become more equal. Here, the extent of power depends on how few alternatives to that relationship the two parties have and how much either party is able to eliminate the alternatives of the other party so that continuing the relationship is less costly than leaving it.

This is very different from the free-market, voluntary relationship in which both parties may choose to withdraw at any time. In this example, at least one of the parties cannot withdraw from the relationship at any time. This is not a market transaction. It does not meet the assumptions of the free-market, rational choice model; therefore, it is social interaction that cannot be turned into an economic transaction *from which both parties draw benefits*. In fact, as the power becomes more balanced, it is possible to realize a situation in which both parties continually increase their costs through the time, energy, and other resources that they devote to harming the other party. This situation is easy to visualize in primary relationships between couples and between offspring and parents, and at the macro level between two ethnic groups warring against each other. However, it also exists in power struggles for top positions in corporations and within interest groups within organizations, such as exist in a single division or subsidiary in which both parties have major investments and no costless alternatives.

Conflict under Conditions of
Unequal Power Distributions

Conflict arises when two actors seek the same goal and cannot attain that goal at the same time, to the same extent (e.g., two parties that cannot hold the same office; two employees who cannot hold the same position; two interest groups of executives in the same firm that cannot control the firm, because one is attempting to become more efficient through expanding research and development and the other through decreasing research and development). One party's goal attainment rules out the other's because they are mutually exclusive; the firm cannot both expand and cut research and development at the same time. The less prone the two parties are to evaluate their gains and losses through economic calculation, the higher the level of conflict.

The economically calculative individual is never committed to a single course of action or a single goal, only to the economic outcomes, the losses and gains. This is what differentiates the social actor from the economic actor, because the substantive ends and the process by which the ends are obtained are more important to the social actor than the economic outcomes. Some social actors do not negotiate easily about the goals (winning or losing the game), whereas others do not negotiate about the process (i.e., participatory democracy) by which the goals are obtained.

RCT attempts to explain conflict by minimizing its effects, because both parties are seen as drawing benefits from the relationship; otherwise, they would not choose to enter into the transaction. However, in many social relationships, both parties do not benefit. One party often gains at the other's expense. That is the situation in a zero sum game. If the resource for which they compete is finite, such as money, a single position, or some other limited resource, one party's gain may be the other's loss.

If parties cannot leave the situation because of closed relationships, they must stay in the relationship and either draw inward or resist the other and attempt to win out. In either case, they are in a power relationship that is, by nature, unequal. The more one party wins out over the other, the less the other will be able to realize his or her interests and attain goals. If neither can exit, the more balanced the power relationship becomes, the more each party will be able to realize its interests and goals approximately midway or half the time if there is agreed-upon cooperation.

The more actors have firm convictions about their goals and appropriate means for reaching them, the less their decision making will be subject to economic calculation, negotiation, and bargaining, and the more it will proceed on the basis of Machiavellian principles, including coercion, threats, mobilization of resources, support through taxes levied on those who are subordinate, threat of withdrawal of affection, claims of legitimacy, and accusations of illegitimacy. Negotiation, bargaining, and economic calculation have little or no place in such power relationships. When the relationship is closed and outcomes are zero sum, a party can win, lose, or be caught in the balance of a draw. Such a relationship cannot be reduced to the maximizing assumptions of an economic transaction.

For this reason, pragmatic politicians are often more long-lived than those committed to specific, nonnegotiable goals. Negotiation, bargaining, and compromise result only where there is a mix of complementary goals. Political actors do not play the game for all-or-nothing but make concessions related to one goal in order to achieve an advantage related to another goal, or they make concessions at one time in exchange for concessions by their negotiating partner at another time. They do not expect, nor can they win, in the sense of completely achieving their goal, but they are better off than if they had totally lost the game. Thus, the political game of negotiation, bargaining, and compromise assumes that there is no rational choice in which the interacting parties both maximize their benefits. They both expect to lose something as they enter the relationship. In the negotiation and bargaining process, many characteristics that are not considered in the rational choice model come into play, such as the actor's commitment to goals, values (ideologies), definitions of acceptable methods of achieving the goals, incentives, legitimacy, and so on. The less an actor is committed to specific goals, and the greater the number of goals, the more flexible the actor can be in the bargaining process; thus, the gains obtained from the process will be greater. However, the more power the party has as it enters the process, the less it will have to make concessions without having to be flexible in its goals.

Not even the decision to be involved in the all-or-nothing game or to be involved in bargaining and negotiation is a rational choice. These decisions are a matter of commitment to goals, social relationships, and the conditions under which the relationship takes place. In bargaining and negotiation processes, the greater gain comes with greater incentives that depend on a party's ability and willingness to make concessions. The wealthier, more flexible party will be able and willing to make more concessions that work as incentives for the other party. Yet the bargaining process takes two parties, and so the wealthier party cannot make more concessions that work as incentives for the other party unless the one party is willing to accept the concessions and make its own concessions in return. The wealthier party would not make concessions without receiving something in return. Thus, bargaining takes place under conditions in which the power distribution over a number of goals or issues is more equal. On the other hand, if the subordinate is committed to specific goals and/or processes, the superordinate will itself have to resort to using more power in order to make gains. Under these conditions, the greater gain comes with greater power. Under conditions of bargaining, the greater gains come with greater incentive offers (often wealth) that act as concessions to the other party. Of course, if there is a show of preexisting power and lack of flexibility on the part of negotiating parties, the relationship can easily turn exclusively into a power game. Negotiation and bargaining enter into the settlement of conflict in power relationships only under the conditions that introduce an economic element, turning the settlement into a bargaining process.

RCT cannot adequately explain power in relationships or in organization. Mayer Zald (1987:705) calls attention to this weakness with reference to the fact that the uses of power are ignored by economic theorists and that the complexity of human behavior is made to appear simple and one-dimensional (Perrow 1981, 1986). Before RCT can be taken seriously in its claim to generalizability and universality, it will have to deal with this fundamental flaw and develop a viable explanation of power.

Authority, Ownership, and Agency

According to the views of RCT, a collective authority will be established and will persist when the number of actors in a system who draw benefits from such an institution increases. The larger the scope of authority, the more those in authority (principals) will be interested in delegating part of their authority to agents. Agents are controlled through drawing benefits from the corporation. Thus, it is to the advantage of the principal for the agent to own shares in the corporation that he or she manages. Coleman (1990) suggests that the more principals and agents cooperate, the more they will identify with each other and trust each other. The more systems of authority delegate responsibility to small units interacting directly with the client or customer, and the more the small units are directly accountable, the more effectively the system of authority will work, which is contrary to a hierarchically organized bureaucracy (Coleman 1990:552-78). This theory seems to integrate authority with economic participation. This is the economics of authority. Yet authority should not be reduced to economics because it has its own unique characteristics. As Simon (1991) points out,

The economies of modern industrialized society can more appropriately be labeled organizational economies than market economies. Thus, even market-driven capitalist economies need a theory of mar-

kets. The attempts of the new institutional economics to explain organizational behavior solely in terms of agency, asymmetric information,
transaction costs opportunism, and other concepts drawn from neo
classical economics ignore key organizational mechanisms like authority, identification, and coordination, and hence are seriously incomplete. (p. 42)

Authority comes as the result of holding a position in an organization (Weber [1947] 1968) and is acquired in many different ways,
including elections, acquisitions, and revolutions. Authority is apparent when those who did not support, vote for, nor fight for the
new administration must nevertheless comply, even though some
may feel that the new administration is unacceptable. A strong and
powerful administration is not like an economic actor who must
constantly provide economic exchanges for compliance. It has the
capacity to enforce decisions that are harmful to employees in the
short run, and sometimes in the long run. The administration draws
its power from multiple and varied sources including wealth, threat
of firing, its reputation among competitors, and its legitimacy among
its public. A comprehensive theory of power must explain not only
the internal but also the external production of power upon which
rests the legitimacy of the organization in its external environment.
Corporations produce and mobilize power just as do executive and
legislative arms of governments. How much power is available for
an individual actor, group, or corporation depends on its ability to
produce and mobilize power both within and outside the organization (Zey-Ferrell 1979; Zey 1993). Trust, support, loyalty, and cooperation between agents are needed in order for willing compliance
with decisions to take place. When these elements are present, potential deviants are less likely to become active.

    A complete explanation of what goes on in power relationships,
authority relationships, and conflict relationships must extend past
economics alone to power from multiple sources. An economics of
power indeed exists, but RCT and its extension to agency theory have
only limited explanatory power beyond economic transactions.

Trust

RCT views trust as based in expected utility and the logic of risk involved (see Coleman 1990:91-115, 175-96). The likelihood of an actor, A, trusting is the product of the value that actor B has for actor A plus the probability with which actor A expects actor B to realize that value in a particular interaction episode. Thus, in RCT, trust depends on how valuable the interaction is and how likely one feels that it will produce gain. The resulting interaction, then, is an economic transaction of trust based on benefits or on expected utility. Consequently, trust is specific to each episode, not built into a relationship.

When trust or mistrust is based on feeling, it may be present at the first encounter with the other party. This trust, or lack thereof, is based in part on past interactions with others who are perceived to have similar attributes. First-sight trust may determine whether or not an actor chooses to interact with another. Thus, feelings of trust act as a selector that contributes to the success of immediate interactions with others. That success in turn serves as an instance in which further trust resides. Trust and mistrust both determine the success of interactions, including economic interactions. If an actor enters a relationship with mistrust, he or she will probably be looking for things that corroborate those feelings. It is much easier to find what one is looking for than what one is not looking for.

In sum, all of these feelings occur before one begins to calculate costs and benefits; they actually shape the subsequent cost-benefit analysis. Essentially, trust and distrust do not work according to the laws of economics but according to the laws of feelings about the familiar and the unfamiliar. However, trust is not necessarily associated with those who are familiar. One may have been exploited by an interaction partner. Thus, others who are like that interaction partner may not be trusted, and others who are unlike this interaction partner may be trusted.

Not only is trust or mistrust built up in continuing relationships with the same actors, but inclinations to trust or mistrust outside of established relationships may also be developed. New experiences can change our assessment of earlier decisions about trust. They call into question earlier feelings, and to change them, the actor must overcome previous learning in that direction. Generally, such barriers are broken down as one repeatedly moves across group, organizational, and societal boundaries or as one moves across racial, ethnic, and national barriers. Of course, this does not mean that economic or moral rationality (value rationality) cannot strengthen trust; however, often what is morally or economically rational may come after and as a result of affective and traditional rationality.

The breaking down of barriers between groups and organizations as well as nations is one of the greatest challenges in building modern societies. Such barriers perpetuate conflict between nations and ethnic, racial, religious, gender, regional, and other groups. In fact, many of these divisions cannot be overcome with zero-sum, economically rational arguments. They are more likely to be overcome by experience or a charismatic leader who can attain the trust of both sides, who represents the importance of the whole, and who demonstrates how both sides can benefit from cooperation—a nonzero sum game that requires negotiation, bargaining, and sometimes altruism.

Altruism

RCT cannot explain altruism because all human action is seen as motivated by selfish, instrumental rationality. This inability to explain altruism has normative implications. Because RCT considers nonrational action morally defective, actors judged nonrational must also be judged ethically deficient.

The theory of rational choice is a normative theory; it tells us what we should do to achieve our aims as well as we can. It does not tell us what our aims should be. It tells us to discard those formally nonrational ethics that fail to adjust means to ends rationally. It is characterized by Weber's "instrumental rationality" (*Zweckrationalität*). It reduces the ethics that a rational person might consider to those alone that are consequentially appropriate. If we all held to this condition of formal rationality with the goal being to "maximize human welfare," the resulting ethic is utilitarianism. The theory of rational choice, then, attributes all actions as "irrational" that do not merely describe the world, and it labels some acts as deviant from the norm of rationality.[1]

RCT is normative in that it stands in judgment over the actor. Given an actor's ends, it will be possible to evaluate whether he or she acted rationally in pursuit of those ends. RCT is empirical in that it claims the ability to explain a course of human action given knowledge (or reasonable imputation) of the utility functions of the actors involved. However, even if one's ends are laudable, to pursue those ends irrationally is ethically defective. According to RCT, people perform altruistic acts not only because they wish to achieve particular ends beneficial to others, but more importantly, because they will maximize their own benefit, either through feeling good about themselves or receiving praise and positive attention from others. If altruistic acts lack self-interest, they are, by RCT's definition, unethical. *How can this be possible?*

Kristen Monroe and her colleagues (Monroe et al. 1990) have suggested that at least some acts of altruism form a class of actors whose motives cannot be accounted for within a rational choice framework. Through intensive interviews with rescuers of Jews in Nazi-occupied Europe, rescuers were distinguished by weak differentiation of individual utilities. In their self-reported motives, they neither acted on the basis of calculation of their own utilities nor formed a weighted average of their own first-order utilities and those on whose behalf they acted. Rather, they tended to dissolve the perception of boundaries between people that make the calculations of individual utilities possible. As one Dutch rescuer put it,

> I was to learn to understand that you're part of a whole, and that just like cells in your own body all together makes your body, that in our society and in our community that we all are like cells of a community

that is very important; . . . you should always be aware that every other
person is basically you. (Monroe 1991a:427)

Monroe aptly calls them John Donne's people, because they are
"strongly linked to others through a shared Humanity. . . . This
self-perception constitutes such a central core to their identity that it
leaves them with no choice in their behavior toward others" (Monroe
1991a:429-30).

As noted, Monroe's work suggests that those who organized to
rescue the Jews in Nazi-occupied Europe did not act as RCT would
have predicted. The normative implication of that prediction is that
they pursued laudable ends through defective means. RCT would
have predicted that Europeans would not shelter the Jews. After all,
it was not in their self-interest to do so. If they did so, they would
surely conclude that to continue to do so in the face of Nazi knowledge of their actions would have been irrational (an evaluation of
means).

Culture and Legitimacy

An economics of culture and legitimacy (Coleman 1990:325-70)
holds that values, attitudes, ideas, cognition, information, and
knowledge are somehow less real than markets and are disseminated
in markets according to rational calculations. That is, actors select
among various values, attitudes, ideas, cognition, info: mation, and
knowledge only because they expect to benefit, choc,ing the least
costly among all options in each and every interaction and turning
them down when their maintenance becomes less rewarding than
alternatives.

Others, including neo-institutionalists, hold that culture and
legitimation cannot be reduced to economics. Some, including Weber
([1947] 1968), hold that whether or not a person holds a given value,
attitude, idea, or knowledge depends more on the meaning and
understanding he or she has for each of these. Criteria, other than

rationality, make actors change their mix of values, attitudes, ideas, or knowledge. An example of one such criterion is *consistency* with the existing cultural mix. When a certain right or authority can be claimed by citizens, organizations, governments, opponents, and other groups and can be justified as legitimate, it can be adopted as a course of action and subsequently maintained against all contradictions of economic rationality.

Race, gender, and labor exploitation are good examples of practices that have been perpetuated by legitimacy and later rationalized as economic. *Legitimacy,* not economic rationality, determines whether groups are allowed by others to proceed in the practice of slavery, racism, sexism, nationalism, and the exploitation of manual labor. To be successful, actors must maintain or sustain validity claims that are broadly accepted among peers, populations, interest groups, classes, race', and genders who have the ability to accept or reject actions. Whether they are able to validate and sustain their claims to legitimacy is dependent on their ability to point to some more generally accepted reasons that are beyond their own particular interests and that coincide with the interests of those who can validate. Part of this argument might appeal to specific economic interests; other parts may claim reasons that have to do with fairness, justice, and rights, whether or *not* an action can be carried out. Citing and appealing only to self-interests seldom results in legitimacy, even in the most self-interested of arenas, such as among bankers. This is a lesson Michael Milken realized when he appealed, all too late, for claims of legitimacy through works of charity. The public was unwilling to accept these claims.

Markets

Markets are made up of relationships, networks of organizations linked together through economic transactions (Mizruchi 1982, 1989), family relationships (Zeitlin 1974), friendships and social clubs (Domhoff 1970, 1974, 1978, 1979, 1983, 1987, 1990), and management circles (Useem 1984, 1993, 1996). These relationships are based on power, authority, conflict, trust, and cooperation, as well as rational economic behavior. Affect, norms, values, knowledge, and information are as much at the basis of these relationships as are economic transactions. Because RCT depends entirely upon an economic interpretation of human behavior, and because markets operate on the basis of relationships, RCT cannot adequately explain the operation of markets. Rational choice theorists solve this fundamental problem by taking markets as an unchallengeable given.

Conclusion

Because RCT comes exclusively out of the thinking realm, and social relationships come, in large part, out of the behavioral realm, RCT cannot deal satisfactorily with a large portion of human interaction. Because the economic transaction is at the heart of rational choice analysis, essentially noneconomic factors elude the rational choice theorist. Because of this restriction, rational choice theorists are forced into casting situations such as spouse abuse in terms of costs and benefits and ignoring those situations where costs over time actually increase. These difficulties occur over a broad range of characteristics of social relationships, making it impossible for RCT to be a unifying social theory.

Note

1. On performatives and quasi-permatives, see J. L. Austin, *How to Do Things with Words*, 2d ed. (Cambridge, MA: Harvard University Press, 1975), and Hanna Fenichel Pitkin, *Wittgenstein and Justice: On the Significance of Ludwig Wittgenstein for Social and Political Thought* (Berkeley: University of California Press, 1972).

CHAPTER 5

Rational Systems of Organization and Rational Choice Economic Theories of Organizations

Rational systems' models of organization posit that organizations are designed specifically to achieve goals, ends, or objectives. These models assume that the achievement of such goals depends on rational means that are achieved through structuring the organization as rationally as possible. In this context, structural rationality is, in the narrow sense, "technical" or "functional" rationality (Mannheim 1950:53). This concept of rationality refers to how a series of actions is organized in such a way as to lead to predetermined goals with maximum efficiency. Thus, rationality refers not to the selection of a goal or multiple goals or to the consistency of the individual's desires and preferences, but to the efficiency of the means used to achieve these goals.

The most valueless, unethical, foolish, illogical goals can be achieved by rational means as well as valuable and ethical goals. As Hannah Arendt (1963) points out, Adolf Hitler's immoral and insane objective of eradicating the European Jewish population was efficiently pursued through efficiently rational means by his administrators, who took the goals as given and worked through efficiently designed means to bring about the extermination of millions of people. Thus, it is important to remember that this, like the rational choice model described in an earlier chapter, is a narrow and restrictive definition of rationality and that it stands in sharp contrast to the broader, substantive rationality defined by Mannheim (1950).

From the rational systems of organizations perspective, individual rationality (i.e., consistency, transitivity, and completeness) is unimportant. What is important is that actions of organizations are performed by purposive agents through efficient means to realize more or less specific goals. Goal specificity is the clearly defined, desired end. Clearly defined, specific goals provide unambiguous criteria for selection among alternative means (strategies and structures) to achieve the specific goals. According to the rational choice model as viewed by economists or decision theorists, goals are translated into a set of preferences or utility functions that represent values of the possible alternative sets of consequences of action. Without clear goals, preference ordering among alternative choices for structures and rational assessment of alternative choices are impossible.

Several organizational theories have been developed that specify how goals support rational behavior in organizations (e.g., see Simon's [1957] classic *Administrative Behavior* and James Thompson's [1967] *Organizations in Action*).

Specific goals are not only criteria for choosing among alternatives, they also guide decisions about how to design organizational structure or form (relationships among organizational entities). Rational structures guide the specification of tasks, as well as the coordination, monitoring, and evaluation of work. In short, rational structures are the processes through which organizational employees are controlled (Zey-Ferrell 1979).

Alvin W. Gouldner (1959) argues that "the rational model implies a 'mechanical' model, in that it views the organization as a structure of manipulable parts, each of which is separately modifiable with a view to enhancing the efficiency of the whole" (p. 405). Organizational structure is viewed solely as a means which can be modified as necessary to improve performance.

The rational systems model deals only with the form of a formalized structure, not with its content. In a formalized structure, positions are specified, roles are defined, and role relationships are prescribed independent of the personal attributes of participants. The content of formal structure has not been of great concern to certain rational systems theorists.

Weber's ([1947] 1968) analysis of administrative structure was only a limited aspect of his much larger interest in accounting for this unique feature of rational Western civilization (see Bendix 1960). In his view, what was distinctive was the growth of rationality in the West, including the United States, which has had an influence on administrative structures. Weber's analysis of organizational structures is lodged firmly in the larger context, as is demonstrated by his differentiation between rational systems characteristics of bureaucrats and of structural characteristics of traditional patrimonial systems controlled by ruler owners. Weber ([1947] 1968:196-204; 329-36) describes the ideal-type bureaucracy as possessing the rational means or structural characteristics listed below, and Richard W. Scott (1981:68-69) contrasts these characteristics with those of patrimonial society.

1. Jurisdictional areas are clearly specified: The regular activities required of personnel are distributed in a fixed way as official duties (in contrast to the patrimonial arrangement, in which the division of labor is not firm or regular but depends on assignments made by the leader that can be changed at any time).

2. The organization of offices follows the principle of hierarchy: Each lower office is controlled and supervised by a higher one. However, the scope of authority of superiors over subordinates is circumscribed, and lower offices enjoy a right of appeal (in contrast to the patrimonial form, where authority relations are more diffuse, being based on personal loyalty, and are not ordered into clear hierarchies).

3. An intentionally established system of abstract rules governs official decisions and actions. These rules are relatively stable and exhaustive, and they can be learned. Decisions are recorded in permanent files. (In patrimonial systems, general rules of administration either do not exist or are vaguely stated, ill-defined, and subject to change on the whim of the leader. No attempt is made to keep permanent records of transactions.)

4. The "means of production or administration"—for example, tools and equipment or rights and privileges—belong to the office, not the office holder, and may include property, working space, and living quarters. (Such distinctions are not maintained in patrimonial administrative systems because there is no separation of the ruler's personal household business from the larger "public" business under his direction.)

5. Officials are personally free; selected on the basis of technical qualifications; appointed to office, not elected; and compensated by salary. (In more traditional administrative systems, officials are often selected from among those who are personally dependent on the leader, such as slaves, serfs, or relatives. Selection is governed by particularistic criteria, and compensation often takes the form of benefices—rights granted to individuals that, for example, allow them access to the stores of the ruler or give them grants of land from which they can appropriate the fees or taxes. Benefices, like fiefs in feudalistic systems, may become hereditary and sometimes are bought and sold.)

6. Employment by the organization constitutes a career for officials. An official is a full-time employee who looks forward to a lifelong career in the agency. After a trial period, he or she gains tenure of position and is protected against arbitrary dismissal. (In patrimonial systems, officials serve at the pleasure of the leader and so lack clear expectations about the future and security of tenure.)

Weber stresses that the administrative system was composed as a multifaceted, interrelated set of structural dimensions. He identifies three types of authority relations: traditional, charismatic, and rational-legal. Weber holds that both the superordinate and subordinates in the power relationship benefit under the rational-legal form because the resulting structure is less capricious and arbitrary than under the other two forms. Specificity of role obligations and clarity of hierarchical connections are defined as rendering stable the system for subordinates. At the same time, the rational-legal structure is touted as providing the possibility for subordinates to have a greater degree of autonomy and freedom because the basis for authority resides in principles and not in personalities and tradition. In addition, the rational-legal structure affords subordinates the flexibility to interpret these impersonal principles. Thomas Spence Smith and R. Danforth Ross (1978) believe that by supporting increased independence and discretion among lower administrative officials, albeit constrained by general administrative policies and specified procedures, bureaucratic systems are capable of handling much more complex administrative tasks than could be managed adequately by traditional and affectively based systems.

Because authority relationships are central to Weber's analysis of rational systems, it is significant that both Parsons (1947:58-60) and Gouldner (1954) have suggested that Weber tended to confuse two analytically distinguishable bases of authority, "incumbency in a legally defined office" and authority "based on technical competency" (Parsons 1947:58-60). Gouldner (1954) points out that Weber states at least once that "bureaucratic administration means fundamentally the exercise of control on the basis of knowledge" (p. 22). This led Gouldner to conclude that

Weber, then, thought of bureaucracy as a Janus-faced organization, looking two ways at once. On the one side, it was administration based on discipline. In the first emphasis, obedience is invoked as a means to an end; an individual obeys because the rule or order is felt to be the best known method of realizing some goal. In his second conception, Weber held that bureaucracy was a mode of administration in which obedience was an end in itself. The individual obeys the order, setting aside judgments either of its rationality or morality, primarily because of the *position* occupied by the person commanding. The content of the order is not examinable. (pp. 22-23)

These are the same only if the place in the hierarchy of a position coincides with the level of knowledge-based technical competency. However, in today's world of small central offices that control multisubsidiary structures, technical competency is lodged at the lowest levels, position-based authority is centralized at the top of the organization, and competency-based power is decentralized. Designation of professional versus technical often delineates these two bases of power.

Similarly, Stanley Udy (1959a, 1959b) was the first organizational analyst to measure Weber's structural characteristics and question Weber's assertion that bureaucratic organizations were necessarily rational (Zey-Ferrell 1979). Udy operationalized the variables (dimensions) that Weber defined in order to measure their interrelationships. Udy drew a sample of 150 organizations from 150 nonindustrialized countries and distinguished the "bureaucratic" attributes of these organizations—the hierarchy of authority and specialization from their rational attributes, including the existence of specified, limited objectives and rewards based on performance. Udy found no association between the two sets of variables: Organizations that possessed more bureaucratic features were not more likely than organizations lacking them to exhibit rational features of goal attainment (Zey-Ferrell 1979). Richard Hall (1963, 1968), Peter Blau and his associates (Blau et al. 1966; Blau and Schoenherr 1971), and Jerald Hage and Michael Aiken (1969) each separately found that an emphasis on technical qualifications (expertise) was negatively correlated with other bureaucratic features such as hierarchy of authority, differentiation of tasks, and formalization of rules and regulations (for further elaboration, see Zey-Ferrell 1979). W. Richard Scott (1981)

(1981) concluded that these findings not only challenge Weber's ideal-type conception of bureaucracy but also lends support to the criticism that "Weber confused authority [of position] with authority of expertise" (p. 73).

Simon (1957:37) differentiates the decisions of individuals in organizations from those a person might be required to make on behalf of an organization. The former is of interest to the rational choice theorist, whereas the latter is of interest to the theorist of organizations as rational systems. Chandler (1962) and Simon (1957) both note that the higher in the organizational hierarchy a decision maker is positioned, the greater the emphasis on values, whereas those decision makers lower in the hierarchy make decisions based more in facts than values. That is, those closer to the top decide what will be done, and those lower down make tactical decisions about how to implement policy decisions made above. The very nature of each type of decision dictates that different criteria be used to determine their suitability. Decisions about goals or ends can be confirmed only by consensus and legitimacy, whereas those about methods can be tested in terms of efficiency after they have been implemented (Simon 1957:45-56).

According to Simon (1957), a scientifically relevant description of an organization details which decisions individuals make as organizational participants. "Goals supply the value premises [that] underlie decisions. Value premises are assumptions about what ends are preferred or desirable" (p. 37). They are combined in decisions with factual premises—assumptions about the relation between means and ends. RCT is applicable only to the latter of the most efficient method of achieving ends. RCT cannot deal with value premises.

Critique of Organizational Economics

I am greatly indebted to the scholarship of and arguments with Lex Donaldson for ideas in this section. For examples of his work, see *American Anti-Management Theories of Organization: A Critique of Paradigm Proliferation* (Donaldson 1995).

The two dominant and highly interrelated organizational economics perspectives in the field of organizational theory are agency theory (Jensen 1989a, 1989b, 1993; Jensen and Meckling 1976; Jensen and Murphy 1990; Jensen and Ruback 1983) and transaction cost economics (Williamson 1975, 1985). These two perspectives were collectively labeled the organizational economics approach by Barney and Ouchi (1986), an approach that has grown in acceptance not only in management departments but also in departments of sociology and economics. As noted by Donaldson (1995), "Oliver Williamson's transaction cost economics received the Irwin Award for Scholarly Contributions in Management at the 1988 Academy of Management National Meeting" (p. 164), and, at the same meeting, Professor Gareth Jones received the award for the best article for his operationalization and empirical analysis of the transaction cost approach, which was published in the *Academy of Management Journal*.

False modesty has never been a limitation of economists. In addition to the passage from the work of Hirschleifer (1986:321) quoted in Chapter 1, which predicted the takeover of the whole of social science, including management organizational analysis, there are other economists, such as Richard E. Caves, who have critically reviewed the research on organizational strategy and structure, business policy, and organizational behavior. Caves (1980) concluded that

> I shall not let professional modesty blur an important conclusion: well-trained professional economists could have carried out many of the research projects cited in this paper more proficiently than did their authors, who were less effectively equipped by their own disciplines. (p. 88)

The intellectual arrogance of economists is not lost on organizational economists, who have otherwise noted that the meager efforts of organizational analysts have been transcended by the theoretically and methodologically more powerful organizational economists (see Jensen 1983, 1993). Also see Hesterly et al. (1990), who wrote, "We argue that OE [organizational economics] has already made an important . . . contribution to our understanding of the nature and purpose of organizations" (p. 403). As noted by Donaldson (1995:165), these scholars advocate that as a result of organizational economics, the prediction of Hirschleifer (1986) will be realized in the field of organizations, namely, that organizational theory will become economics as part of the development of what Barney (1990:389) terms "economic imperialism."

Lex Donaldson (1995) offers the following descriptions of agency and transaction cost theory:

Agency theory holds that organizations can be analyzed in terms of a conflict of interest between principals and agents (Jensen and Meckling 1976). Particularly in the large modern corporation, the principals of the organizations are the owners, the many outside shareholders, who own but delegate control to the executive managers who are their agents (Eugene F. Fama and Jensen 1983). Managers have interests . . . which diverge from those of the principals and so may use their discretion to maximize their interests at the expense of the interests of the principals—this is termed residual loss (Jensen and Meckling 1976:308). Such residual loss can be curbed to a degree through various devices such as monitoring and sanctioning, including control over executives by a non-executive board of directors (Fama and Jensen 1983). Agency theory tends to see managers as ever ready to cheat the principals or owners unless constantly controlled in some way. Transaction cost theory holds that market failure occurs such that the normal economic pressure on economic actors to perform effectively breaks down and has to be replaced by hierarchical controls. In the large corporation with a multi-level hierarchy, middle managers enjoy a degree of independence from top management and begin to subordinate the corporate goals of the maximization of profit and shareholder wealth in favor of their personal self-aggrandizement. The solution is to increase control on middle managers by holding them directly accountable for the profitability of their division as assessed by an investigatory control staff of head-office accountants and the like, that is, the M-form corporation (Williamson 1970, 1971, 1981, 1985). (pp. 165-66)

When one corporation is in the process of purchasing merchandise from another, haggling over price is common. The avoidance of transaction costs associated with such negotiations is attained by recourse to administration of both transacting parties through a common hierarchy. According to Williamson (1975, 1981, 1985) and Alchian and Woodward (1988), greater efficiency is achieved by a merger of the two firms or acquisition of one by the vertically integrated process. The duplicity and untrustworthiness of managers in the two firms is resolved by placing a common boss over them and eliminating conflict (for further elaboration, see Donaldson 1995:166).

Thus, the nature of one manager is somehow more trustworthy and less opportunistic than the nature of two managers, and the nature of managers is inherently more untrustworthy and opportunistic than that of boards controlled by owners. The explanation for these assumptions are never laid bare by organizational economists. Donaldson (1995) shows that the label "organizational economics" is rhetorical in that the models are less economically based than their proponents would like the reader to think, and by attaching it to themselves, they hope to attain the superior status that they claim among organizational analysts.

Organizational Economics
and the Unit of Analysis

Unlike most organizational theories, which focus on the organization as the unit of analysis, economic theories of organizations are based on the individual as the unit of analysis—a particular type of individual, one who is competitively self-interested. Like RCT, which claims to subsume all other social sciences (see Chapter 1), economic theories of organizations, such as agency and transaction cost theory, claim to supplant the otherwise defective field of organizational theory (Barney 1990).

Although agency theory and transaction cost theory are relatively new, they find their roots in the early organizational theory of Chester Barnard's (1938) writing on inducements, contribution calculus, and individual decision making in organizations. They also draw on the first part of James March and Herbert Simon's *Organizations* (1958), in which rational individuals decide if they will become affiliated with the organization, and once becoming affiliated, decide if they will work or shirk.

ONE ORGANIZATION EQUALS ONE PERSON

For assumptions of competitive self-interest to be applicable to organizations, economic organizational theories based on RCT's premises must assume that multinational organizations that are made up of multiple departments, divisions, and subsidiaries are unified in their motives. That is, the dubious assumption is made that organizations can be treated as single people or as entrepreneurs. The organization operates as a single person who gathers information and resources, produces goods and services, and makes decisions about what will maximize utility (profits). This conception ignores the complexity of organizations with all their forms, levels, human motives, conflicts, and actions.

The economic organization theorist sees the organization as existing in name only. This nominalist view allows for the summarial dismissal of the importance and control that the collective, especially the organization, has in constraining individual choice and subsequent behavior. In contrast, organizational theorists view the organization as real; they take its power and ability to constrain human actions seriously. In fact, they see the organization as defining values, and groups and organizations as influencing preferences and action.

Organizational theorists undoubtedly argue that the basic structure of motivation is learned and is not inherent to humans, as rational choice assumes. Motivations, they argue, are learned in the course of social action and redefined in subsequent actions, not given a priori; they also change within the context of each collective situation.

THE ORGANIZATION AS A MARKET

Economic organizational theorists deal with exchanges, specifically exchanges in free capitalist markets. They assume that organizations function as perfectly competitive, profit-seeking markets. For example, Williamson (1975) defines the origin of organizations (hierarchies) as the reduction of transaction costs through internal control of resources and markets for products. Under conditions of equilibrium of perfect competition and a perfect market, large profits of a few organizations will attract many other organizations until the profits are equally spread among them, producing a market equilibrium, until new products, technologies, markets, and so on, disturb it. These models ignore conditions of incomplete information, inadequate distribution of information, inadequate resources, unfair market practices, secrecy and deception in the transfer of technologies, and coercion of one organization by another.

The organization operates as a market, and it operates in a perfectly competitive market. It produces goods, and the market decides if it will survive. Yet we know that often, other organizations, including competitors, decide if an organization will survive (Zey 1993). We also know that organizations do not just produce their products for acceptance or rejection by the market, they form strategies and products control not only their acceptance but the volume and price at which competitor's products are accepted, as well as the volume and price at which their competitors are accepted in the market.

Presumably, if the firm produced a better product at a lower cost, that product would, with certainty, be accepted by the market. Yet we know that automatic acceptance does not take place. For corporations in a growth sector, predicting market changes and uncertainty must take into account the effects of government regulations and the strategies of competitors. What are the consequences of unevenly distributed resources, incomplete information, inaccurate information, volatile environments, and other circumstances for organizational certainty? Obviously, they are enormous. For example, organizational theorists ask if there are facts that lie outside the economic exchange that are important. Of course, even in the study of economic exchange, there are many factors of great importance that lie outside the realm of economists' strictly defined, "rational" action, such as new and amended laws, war, and elections.

By excluding attention to nonrational elements of human behavior, organizational economists leave themselves little ability to explain changes in human behavior and social structure and no way of learning about the world outside their limited model. In addition, they leave themselves little ability to explain group and organizational actions that are based on negotiation and compromise. This overly rational worldview may lead to the exclusion of the noneconomic aspects of organizational experience and functioning. Organizational analysts are open to the possibility of rational action, but they do not exclude social structure, culture, and emotion as bases of action at individual, group, and organizational levels of action.

Power in Organizational Economic Theory versus Power in Theories of Organizations

Rational choice and organizational economic theories completely disregard power in exchange situations. Yet power exists in all exchanges. Typical formulations of the basis of power are those of John French and Bertram Raven (1968) and the resource dependence theory of Pfeffer (1992). Like RCT, these models often assume perfect knowledge on the part of all actors to judge correctly the utility of all resources in all situations. Such assumptions are without warrant; they are not even guaranteed within the ideological practice of capitalistic society.

The major limitation of this type of organizational economic theory is that such models begin with each party possessing some unknown, predetermined resource base. A theory of power ought to include an exposition of how some people come to have access to these "resources" and others do not. The prior possession of resources in anything other than equal amounts is something that a theory of "power" has to explain. This is especially true of RCT, which presumes that both parties maximize, and that somehow equilibrium is achieved. How does this equilibrium come about? RCT should justify its presumption in some way. Prior and inequitable distributions of resources are taken for granted in both organizational economic theory and RCT.

Conclusion

Rational systems of organization theory is concerned with the formal structure of organizations and not with the interaction of the various elements of organizations. It focuses on the efficient accomplishment of ends rather than the actual ends themselves, and it sees the rational structure of the organization as the way it controls employees.

Max Weber was very interested in the growth of rationality in the United States and analyzed administrative structure as part of his larger work on rational western civilization. Later researchers found that Weber did not distinguish between authority vested in a position or office and authority that comes from specialized knowledge or technical expertise. Such distinctions are crucial to the workings of modern corporations and are becoming more critical because of the growth in technological knowledge in the past two decades.

Complex organizations such as corporations are of great interest to economists, organizational theorists, rational choice theorists, and others. Two relatively recent theories that have their roots in early organizational theory, but use many of the approaches of economic theory, are agency theory and transaction cost theory. Taken together, they comprise a subfield known as organizational economics. Most organizational theories analyze the whole organization, but organizational economic theory, like RCT, concerns itself only with the individual, who is assumed to be competitively self-interested at all times. In addition, when organizational economic theorists do consider the organization as a whole, they conceive of it as if it were an individual. To do this, much of the natural complexity of large organizations is ignored.

Organizational economic theorists see organizations as functioning like markets, but only in an ideal model where equilibrium between markets and competitors prevails. By excluding all but rational elements, organizational economic theorists are unable to explain changes or action based on the give-and-take that occurs in real-world environments. As a result, power and access to resources, especially capital, remain unexplained by RCT and organizational economic theory alike. Such fundamental characteristics of capitalist organizations should not be overlooked by any social theory. In contrast, organizational theorists include rational elements and elements such as culture and structure in their analyses of the workings of large social structures. In spite of the shortcomings of social theories based solely in economics, proponents claim that organizational theory is defective and will be absorbed and replaced by rational organizational economic theory.

CHAPTER 6

Criticisms of
Rational Choice Models[1]

*The problem is that the assumptions underlying the economic
model are not only very simple, they are also very strong and
wildly unrealistic. . . . The cost is that economic policy premised
on [such] simple assumptions often leads to unintended—and
dysfunctional—consequences. (Bower 1983:181)*

In summary, I will examine the major criticisms of rational choice
theory (RCT) by drawing from my previous work (Zey 1992) and my
reviews of the work of Coleman (Zey 1994). In the United States, the
impact of rational choice models on the social sciences has acceler-
ated over the past 20 years. It began in earnest with the oil crisis of
1973 and has been perpetuated by the conservative political admin-
istrations of Reagan and Bush. Other countries in the western
world—Britain, under the leadership of Margaret Thatcher, and Germany, led by Helmut Kohl, as well as Eastern Europe—have moved
away from welfare states, collective interests, and concern for labor

and toward interests of corporate capitalism. These transformations have reinforced the similar changes taking place in the United States. Using rational choice logic, many types of organizations—corporations, public bureaucracies, and voluntary associations—are being subjected to economic analysis in attempts to make them accountable or productive or competitive. Resources are redistributed from the public to the private sector, and, in return, private associations are asked to pick up the slack in funding social services. At the same time, the public sector is being dismantled, individualism is experiencing a resurgence. Throughout the 1980s and 1990s, the executive branch and the Rehnquist court rejected pleas for civil rights and economic equality, and institutionalized values that support individual interests, utility maximization, and cost accounting. Neoclassical economics and its variations have provided both the rationales and the methods. Many social scientists followed the lead of neoclassical economics and embraced variants of public choice theory, RCT, expected utility theory and, in organizational analysis, TCA and agency theory, as evidenced in the work of Hirschleifer (1986).

Although rational choice models use an economic metaphor, they are theoretically generalized to explain not only economic behavior but also the behavior studied by nearly all social science disciplines, from political choice to psychology. The range of human behavior explained encompasses the entire spectrum, including government decision making (Allison 1971); individual consumer decisions (Becker 1976); collective economic agents (Allison and Szanton 1976); social institutions such as the criminal justice system (Becker 1968; Ehrlich 1973) and the family (Becker 1981); and social behavior in general (Becker 1976). The data are viewed as consistent with rational choice models with the exception of certain errors of the flesh, human weaknesses and frailties, and other so-called "minor exceptions." The anomalies of unwise, value-laden, altruistic, emotion-based decisions do not limit the theory of rational choice for its most committed adherents. Evidence that the rationality of decisions is blocked by emotions, as demonstrated by Holsti's (1979) finding that one's capacity for rational decisions may seriously decline in situations of high stress, is negated by rational choice theorists. In addition to the limitations of individuals, some people, alone or by using organizations, act fraudulently. Are both deviant and normative behavior rational? If not, which one is, and how is the other explained by the rational choice calculus? Is the other simply irrational?

Other scholars within the social sciences see the inability of the neoclassical model to explain both individual-level phenomena, such as the origins of individual preferences and the complexities of choice, as well as macrolevel phenomena, such as collective actions and nonmarket allocative systems. Students of social organizations and complex organizations alike have begun to challenge the neoclassical models.

In analyzing the various criticisms made of the dominant approach to the study of decision making, RCT, it became clear that these criticisms originated not only from those who have used these approaches, but also from alternative perspectives. Although criticism has originated from within and without the dominant paradigm, no single work has explored every criticism. Typically, each has focused on one or more points. Because critiques are launched from a variety of perspectives, they recommend a variety of alternative solutions to the limitations of the dominant perspective. These recommendations are diverse, contradictory, and only partially developed. There exists no comprehensive review of these criticisms and no thorough critique of the entire writing of a single author who writes from a "rational choice" perspective.

To preface the critiques presented, I offer the qualification that not all theorists who write from the dominant approach have adopted all the assumptions, characteristics, and methodologies elaborated below. Not all theorists who write from the dominant perspective accept these assumptions, characteristics, and methodologies with equal vigor (e.g., some researchers have focused on decision making under various forms of uncertainty with a prominent place for questions of utility assessment, probability assessment, and risk assessment [Edwards and Tversky 1967]). Other theorists have attempted to compensate for deficiencies in the current paradigm (Ulen 1983:576) with rational choice-consistent alternatives such as "transaction cost analysis" (Olson [1965] 1971; Williamson 1981, 1985), "agency theory" (Jensen 1983), and "rational expected utility theory" (Fischoff, Goitein, and Shapira 1981; von Neumann and Morgenstern 1947). For similar criticisms of the neoclassical model, see Rubin (1983:719) and Simon (1987).

This critique examines the following assumptions underlying rational choice theories:

1. The individual is antecedent to and independent of the group.

2. Humans are only self-interested.

3. Humans act only out of rationality.

4. Value is subjective.

5. Humans are utility maximizing.

6. Utility is subjective.

7. The neoclassical view is value neutral.

8. The individual is the appropriate unit of analysis.

9. Organizations function rationally.

10. Organizations function efficiently.

11. Power and conflict are limited.

1. THE INDIVIDUAL IS ANTECEDENT TO AND INDEPENDENT OF THE GROUP

Individual behavior is the independent variable in rational choice models. Separate individuals are defined as rationally self-interested maximizers of utility prior to the existence of any group. They are born with a nature that is largely Hobbesian. The collective does not determine the individual, as in functional theory, where the individual is born tabula rasa (with a clean slate) and socialized into society. The individual exists before and causes the collective. Individual action is the basic explanation (Wallace 1980) of all social organization.

But what if "others" constrain individual decisions? Choices are interdependent in at least four ways. First, for the sake of the rational choice argument, we will pretend for a moment that humans act rationally and have a single utility function. Rational choice models assume that individual choices are independent of one another. They fail to acknowledge that our utility may be a result not only of our own welfare but also of the welfare of those for whom we care. If we increase our personal welfare by decreasing theirs, we will be less well-off. Thus, a given choice has implications not only for self, but for self through others. A second form of interdependence is that utility and value may depend on the extent to which others prefer the service or good. For example, the value of rank or status increases as others value it. Even money has symbolic value (Lane 1991). Third, our choices may cause others to constrain our future choices. If we increase our share of the proverbial pie, our ruthless egoistic interests may cause the reprisal of others in the future. Thus, our present choices as well as our future choices are dependent on others. Threat of reprisal may act as a deterrent to independent maximization. Fourth, not all outcomes are zero-sum. Thus, with regard to some resources, we can enhance our self-interest only by enhancing that of others. As one member of the group gains influence, so do other members, as a function of acting collectively or as a function of shared status (see Bacharach and Lawler 1980).

Social embeddedness and institutional theorists argue that humans both create and are products of social interaction. Habits of mind and behavior develop in a social and cultural context. Intellect guides conduct; choices are judged by references to consequences. Humans are thinking, choosing, judging individuals (Strauss 1978). For comparison, we offer the sociocultural person whose motivations are multiple and complex, whose intellect can and will change the human condition as he or she emerges and discriminates.

2. HUMANS ARE ONLY SELF-INTERESTED

Rational choice assumes that humans make only self-interested decisions. These self-interested humans are separately and economically rational. This means (Green 1981:14-15) that they have reflexive, transitive, and complete orderings of preferences. Preferences are based on these orderings. Humans seek maximal and efficient satisfaction of their own preferences. Each knows that all other humans are economically rational maximizers. Knowing this, each seeks the maximal and efficient satisfaction of his or her own preferences.

The underlying question of what motivates human behavior is explainable by one basic motive: self-satisfaction or pleasure. But is it not more complex than this? Are humans ever torn between increasing self-satisfaction and commitment to others? What if some are not just self-interested but also other-interested? What if altruism is as valid a basis for action as self-interest? What if fairness is a consideration?

For the theory to be testable, preferences must be stable and a consistent (and presumably perfect) relationship must exist between preferences and behavior, because preferences are "revealed" by the actor's previous actions. Assuming preferences to be stable allows previous choices (behavior) to be taken as indicative of current and future preferences and to be measured as such. Margaret Mooney Marini (1992) argues that using behavior as a measure of past preferences does not allow for changes in preferences (attitudes) or for the possibility of behavioral modification resulting from such changes. David Willer (1992) argues against the assumption of stable preferences on other grounds. Furthermore, Marini views as tautological the supposition that people choose what they value and that what they value is revealed only by what they choose.

I argue that moral and emotional acts have fundamentally different sources of valuation and explanations of the reasons people act than those provided by RCT, which is based in consumptive pleasures and maximization of profits. Morality and affect are different bases of behavior from that of pleasure. If we analyze all actions (those based in values, affect, and means-ends) as though they are simply sources of pleasure, satisfaction, or any other source of preference, we will overlook the differences between rational action based on pleasure and moral commitment, the expression of emotional feelings, and habit.

3. HUMANS ACT ONLY OUT OF RATIONALITY

All social scientists agree that humans have reasons for what they do. Therefore, reasonableness is not in question—it is what constitutes rationality that is in question. Furthermore, whether rationality is the *only* basis for action is also in question. Although there are numerous definitions of rationality used by the disciplines of economics, psychology, sociology, and political science, neoclassical economists differ from these other social scientists in their definition. Economists use the term *irrationality* (nonrational) very broadly to designate any behavior that cannot be construed to fit the rational choice models (e.g., Becker 1962). Also, they use the term *rationality* very narrowly to exclude action based on emotion, habit, and values (for a discussion, see Simon 1987). The neoclassical model defines choice as rational *if the outcome is rational*. All behavior that does not produce the rational outcome is irrational. In the other social sciences, the conceptualization of decision making is rational because of the process it employs. The rational choice models rest on consistency of individuals' logic, whereas the other social sciences concentrate on procedural rationality of collectives and organizations.

Although early rational choice models contained premises that behavior is motivated by egoism, hedonism, or self-interest, more recently, economists have defined rational action as the choice that conforms to the actors' preferences and has utility. Any preference is assumed to have utility. Defining rationality as the actors' preferences by definition makes all behavior rational. That a person's behavior is rational is irrefutable when inferred from that person's preferences. Thus, instead of the action being an outgrowth of the utility, and therefore rational, the logic is turned on its head, and a person's choice to behave or perform an act is used as justification for its utility and therefore its rationality. Furthermore, Marini (1992) challenges the assumption that preferences are unchanging and exogenous to the process of choice. Specifically, she challenges assumptions of cancellation, transitivity, dominance, and invariance.

Preferences are inferred from choices. The problem, however, is that an imaginative analyst can construct an account of value-maximizing choice for any action or set of actions performed (Allison 1971:35). In fact, preferences are constructed after the fact as explanations of decisions (choices). These preferences become the needs or goals of individuals that would be consistent with their decisions. Of course, these preferences, being assumed, cannot be falsified. Indeed, the ability of researchers to construct such preferences, post hoc, to account for previously observed decisions, makes RCT very attractive to those who are predicting action but are not interested in the extent to which their theory corresponds to actual preferences of actors.

For many sociologists, political scientists, and especially psychologists, this broad definition of rationality lacks specificity. They replace it with the narrower maximization of expected utility models (von Neumann and Morgenstern 1947). Most social scientists agree that behavior can be judged rational only in the *frame* in which it takes place (Simon 1979; Tversky and Kahneman 1987). The frame consists of goals, definitions of the situation, and computational resources.

The social sciences have a long, rich history of writings on rationality. In the tradition of neoclassical economic science, as in the writings of Vilfredo Pareto (1935), an action is rational when it corresponds with the ends or goals sought. Rationality means the adaptation of means to ends. The more congruent the means to the ends, the more efficient the decision and, therefore, the more rational the organization (Weber [1947] 1968). Economists abstain from applying the test of rationality to ends. They assume rationality if the outcome is obtained efficiently. *Formal rationality* (*Zweckrationell* [Weber (1947) 1968]), *logical action* (Pareto 1935), and *instrumental rational action* (Parsons and Shils 1951) all designate relationships in which means are adapted to desired ends—the type of relationship at the basis of rational choice models. Weber introduced a second type of rational action that is based in values (*Wertrationell*). Formal rationality refers to the given ends or goals that are achieved, and value rationality refers to which ends are chosen in the first place. Rational choice models deal with the first and not the second type of rationality.

Neoclassical economists model the formally rational actions of individuals. When they are faced with variant choices made by decision makers, they are disturbed because rational choices *should be* invariant. When presented with contrary evidence, neoclassical economists rationalize or discredit the evidence. Fallibilities of economic actors are assumed to be random rather than systematic and therefore not of interest to economists. The interests of other social scientists lie in the extent and nature of the variants, in most cases. When means and ends are not in agreement, those who work from the rational choice perspective try to explain the lack of concordance between the objectives sought and the results obtained as unexpected or latent consequences (Merton 1936), unforeseeable results (Allison 1971), and uncertainty (Kahneman, Slovic, and Tversky 1982; Tversky and Kahneman 1974). A second way in which they explain incongruencies is to analyze the inconsistencies in the process. Some social science disciplines focus on constructing models of the processes by which rational decisions should be made. They are interested in variant preferences and what leads to them. These variant preferences may be due to ambiguity about probabilities (Einhorn and Hogarth 1987), framing variance (Tversky and Kahneman 1981), and inadequate feedback to enable learning (Tversky and Kahneman 1987:90-91). A third explanation of variants is what cognitive and social psychologists have labeled "systematic errors" of scientific, objectively rational models of decision making.

Habit, values, and emotions are bases for the selection of not only ends but also means in economic, political, and social decision-making processes. People use at least four heuristics that generate different bases of decisions. First, according to the availability heuristic, they depend on salient information that is easily retrievable from memory. Camic (1986) calls this *habit*. Second, according to the representativeness heuristic, they act as if stereotypes are more common than they actually are. Third, according to the anchoring heuristic, they let their judgments rely on some initial value (see Etzioni's [1986, 1988] work on the moral dimension; also see Marini [1992]). The fourth heuristic of acting out of emotions is being explored enthusiastically (e.g., see Scheff 1992). Also see Max Bazerman (1986) for what he calls *judgment mistakes* related to these four heuristics. These "errors" are documented frequently in the research as outside rational decision making, or as errors and anomalies that must be plastered over to repair the models. I argue that they are alternative bases of human behavior.

Even if we assume that humans have complete information, that they act without regard for the preferences of others and only in their self-interest, that they have a single set of unambivalent preferences, and that they enter every choice with the intention of maximizing utility, they still do not act rationally. Psychologists have shown that humans are more likely to accept a risk option that is framed as gains than one framed as losses; they are more likely to place a high value on a human cost if they know those who will incur it; and they are more likely to estimate a high probability of a random event if they are given a high baseline than if they are given an equally low baseline (Frank 1990; Tversky and Kahneman 1974). Humans do not always make rational choices.

4. VALUE IS SUBJECTIVE

What is good for an individual is defined by his or her preferences, desires, and wants. Value is subjective because it is defined as individual preferences and therefore varies from individual to individual. There may be preferences that are held in common, but they are not collective preferences for collective good. They are subjective in the sense that there is no objective order or externalized moral standard against which to assess the worth of preferences. Thus, there is no immutable set of values that all men and women must pursue or that guide preferences or desires. This subjectivity prevents the formation of social values and a moral order. Values have to arise from the individual preferences of actors. Therefore, any relationship is undermined by the tenets of rationality. A relationship must exist between agents that would generate cooperation necessary for a postulated agreement. Commitment, solidarity, and trust are relational and do not exist in nonrelationships. If actors trust each other, they can establish an agreement. But trust itself is a relationship between individuals and cannot be presupposed without violating the tenets of RCT. Trust (because it occurs within a relationship) must be explained by RCT, not assumed or presupposed. The dilemma is that rational actors cannot create the relationship of trust because this relationship would be useful for each actor rather than in each individual's self-interest alone. In originating relationships, the actors must have trust or some form of solidarity to underpin the exchange. But according to RCT, which assumes self-interested maximizers, there are no values within the individual or forces external to the individual sufficient to make actors keep their commitment or trust. Trust is impossible to establish without some external set of values. (See Durkheim [1890] 1973, [1905] 1977, [1895] 1982 for classical explanations, and see Kanter [1972]; Ouchi [1981]; and Shapiro [1987] for more macro-oriented explanations of the importance of trust to organizational functioning. Also see Donaldson [1990a, 1990b] for a different critique of TCA's formulation of trust)

5. HUMANS ARE UTILITY MAXIMIZING

RCT treats all social systems as markets at or near equilibrium, a highly restrictive scope. Willer (1992) argues that for most organizations, the content of value is restricted inappropriately to utility measured in economic terms. RCT assumes that alternatives are evaluated according to their effects on final wealth levels. Marini (1992) marshals empirical evidence to support the opposing view that options are assessed in terms of gains and losses relative to some reference point. She also amasses empirical evidence to demonstrate that the utility or value function is nonlinear. James Bohman (1992) contends that economic utility is not the only end of action and that RCT can explain only economic action.

Establishing utility and probability as axioms in a theory of choice behavior assumes that individuals have the knowledge and computational ability to determine alternatives and their consequences. It further assumes certainty in present and future evaluations of consequences and holistic evaluation of alternatives based on a consistent measure of utility. Marini (1992) argues that research on perception, recognition, and information storage and retrieval supports a "bounded rationality" view of limited information-processing capabilities.

Arguments against the mono-utility and in support of the multi-utility assumption for the motivation of human actors have their bases in definitions of rationality. The neoclassical economic assumption that human action is based only on functional means-ends relationships filters out the effects of values, emotions, and other bases of actions. Hans E. Jensen (1987) argues that neoclassical economists have developed the idea that humans are fixed, final, and given to utility maximization. Neoclassical theorists see utility as the basic unit of all human preferences and profit maximization as the ultimate individual goal. Neoclassical theories that assume that managers are aiming at profit maximization are different from those that assume that organizational managers are seeking satisfactory profits as well as other organizational goals. Most of the analysis of organizational decision making assumes that economic agents seek to increase utility, but other organizational goals not only exist but are sometimes given greater priority than profit maximization.

Through the analysis of the works of several neoclassical economists, Simon (1987) finds that neoclassical economists make a wide
range of auxiliary empirical assumptions in order to preserve the
utility-maximizing paradigm, even when the supporting assumptions are unverified and, in some cases, unverifiable.

> When verification is demanded, they tend to look for evidence that the
> theory makes correct predictions and resist advice that they should look
> instead directly at the decision mechanisms and processes. [It fails to
> observe that] the force of its predictions derives from the usually
> untested, auxiliary assumptions that describe the environment in
> which decisions are made. (pp. 38-39)

In criticizing the normative model of RCT, Simon (1987) asserts that
neoclassical economists hold that economic actors always reach the
decision that is "objectively, or substantively, best for the given utility
function" (p. 27). As constructed and defended, neoclassical theory
is both tautological and irrefutable. I contend with Bohman (1992)
that economic utility is not the only end of action and that RTC can
explain only economic action.

Rational choice models are insensitive to cognitive limitations
possessed by individuals and organizations (Simon 1979). Simon
emphasized the concept "boundedly rational decision making" (Simon 1957), which recognizes the limitations of the information-processing capacities of individuals and organizations in making decisions (Simon 1976). *Satisficing* in decision making means that actors
stop the search when they find a satisfactory alternative. This is a
more valid explanation than maximizing or optimizing because time
constraints, framing problems, and human limitations prohibit maximizing and optimizing. But researchers have been unable to opera-
tionalize the concept of satisficing. Humans cannot maximize because they are not totally rational (discussed above) and because they
cannot fully implement the rational process. They cannot obtain
complete information even before making important decisions. All
possible alternatives are not known, and outcomes attached to each

alternative are not obvious. Gathering full information is too costly. Because they do not have complete information and cannot predict fully the results of their decisions, those decisions will be suboptimal. Actors have simpler and more uncertain maps of the domain of their decision than is likely to be optimal. Because the information search is limited, the accurate probabilities of various outcomes will be less important to the choices made than the inaccurate probabilities that the decision makers perceive. Objective values cannot be placed on all the consequences of choices, so the subjective values (utilities) of the actor prevail. Instead of considering all alternatives, actors consider only those alternatives that are readily definable, of which there are a small number—only enough to find a satisfactory solution to the problem. Marini (1992) reduced the assumption that humans act (rationally) to maximize or optimize returns to the assumption that they act to produce beneficial results. Marini then marshals empirical evidence to support the view that options are assessed in terms of gains and losses relative to some reference point.

6. UTILITY IS SUBJECTIVE

Evidence negating the fact that humans act in means-ends-related ways is dismissed in several ways. One is to explain nonrational behavior by invoking whatever source of utility is needed to rationalize that particular behavior. This is possible within the theory because utility, subjectively defined, is different from objective value. Thus, if I were to posit that some action is based on emotions, a plausible position for a proponent of rational choice would be to argue that the emotion has some utility. Furthermore, if the emotion is a good feeling, it can be defined as having utility and therefore being rational. Thus, a person might act against his or her self-interest and in the interest of another person because it makes the person feel good, which has utility and is therefore rational. If we assume that feeling good is pleasurable and has utility, it is in the actor's self-interest. If we take this one step further, we can explain an altruistic act as being in the actor's self-interest. Because neither self-interest nor utility is measured—both are assumed—there is no way to refute the utility assumption. Altruistic behavior, which is nonrational, is by rational choice definition a particularly subtle form of self-interest. How does one explain actions that are self-damaging as utility producing? Because of the subjective definition of utility that is post facto for the action, nothing prevents the researcher from attributing utility to self-damaging or altruistic behavior. Thus, people who stay in destructive relationships are described as rational by assuming that they receive utility from the abuse that they experience. Altruism and masochism are thereby both reduced to rational choices.

If altruism, masochism, trust, and other such phenomena cannot be dissolved into subtle forms of self-interested utility maximization, a broader and more complex definition of the bases of human behavior is necessary. Proponents of rational choice may wish to consider that other bases of behavior are legitimate. Broadening the definition of rational behavior (see Elster 1979, chap. 3) to include all bases of behavior in fact confounds the problem. Recognition of affective, valuative, and habitual bases of action would help social scientists to explain wider ranges of human behavior.

7. NEOCLASSICAL VIEW IS VALUE NEUTRAL

Neoclassical economics is the only social science discipline that still clings to the assumption of value neutrality. Other social science disciplines dispelled such myths a quarter of a century ago (Gouldner 1970). Disagreeing with Kurt Klappholz (1984), Gunnar Myrdal points out, "Valuations are always with us. . . . Our valuations determine our approach to a problem, the definition of concepts, the choice of models, the selection of observations . . . in fact, the whole pursuit of study from beginning to end" (1979, p. 148). For example, the rational choice models ask questions about how to maximize efficiency or growth. They do not realize that efficiency, productivity, and growth are values. The emphasis on efficiency as the basis of rational choice models values self-serving, individualized choice over collective choice and public goals (Solo 1981). Neoclassical economists fail to ask questions concerning whose interests are served by the values underpinning the rational choice model. Questions of entitlement, rights, power, distribution of wealth, and status are assumed uncritically to be the result of productivity, when in fact they may be the product of inheritance, accident, graft, fraud, or embezzlement.

In using the rational choice model, decision making and problem solving are accomplished through market mechanisms that drastically limit whose interests count and whose do not (Hickerson 1987; Samuels 1981). Priority of efficiency over other values limits questions of the legitimacy of the present order. Measuring efficiency as the net of outputs minus inputs is a reflection of the status quo distribution of entitlements and rights. Such premises are biased in support of the status quo. Economists believe that high profits for owners should be increased; this is evidence of efficiency, and efficiency benefits society because resources are saved. This situation allows theories that explain economic behavior to also serve as normative prescriptions for how society *should be*. Transaction cost economics similarly argues that the present economic distribution is the most efficient way to produce goods and services for an industrial society, thus supporting the status quo for those who control the present distribution.

Because the purpose of an enterprise economy is to facilitate the satisfaction of wants, orthodoxy effectively recommends that *what is* is the standard or criterion for judging *what ought to be* (Tool 1986). Hickerson (1987) concludes, "Thus orthodoxy's 'positive' perception of 'is' becomes also its normative, and status-quo biased, prescription of 'ought'" (p. 1123). The ability of self-labeled, economic organizational theorists to recognize the value premises of their critics (see Barney's [1990] analysis of Perrow's work) but not their own biases may be due to the orthodox, positive perspective and its status quo bias. Such political biases may be more easily visible from outside than from inside rational choice perspectives (Donaldson 1990b:395).

8. THE INDIVIDUAL IS THE APPROPRIATE UNIT OF ANALYSIS

The debate concerning the appropriate unit of analysis has been long and enlightening. This debate has come recently to organizational analysis (see Zey-Ferrell 1981 and Donaldson 1985). Adherence to the selection of the individual as the unit of analysis by rational choice and transaction cost analysts is labeled "reductionist" in contemporary critiques. These critics cite structuralist and collectivist views of organizations as alternatives. These views are as old as the discipline of sociology and are championed by structuralists from Blau (1970; Blau and Schoenherr 1971) to Granovetter (1985) and Coleman (1984). The strongest view of organizations is that they are made up of relationships (Coleman 1984; Granovetter 1985). Relationships are different from aggregated phenomena because relationships signify interaction between actors in the organization, and not merely that actors are located in a common unit that is designated by the researcher. Network analysis has substantially increased our understanding of relationships within and among organizations.

I argue that social collectives—dyads, primary groups such as voluntary associations and families, and complex organizations such as private enterprises and public bureaucracies—are more likely than individuals to be decision-making units. Decisions are most frequently made by groups within the context of larger social collectives. Organizational theory holds that when people assume organizational positions, they adapt to the roles, positions, goals, and values of the organization. Organizational power structures, communication networks, and other patterns of information flow influence decision making. Furthermore, organizations have varying degrees of success in accepting and assimilating information from the environment, especially if that environment is unknown, hostile, or ill-defined. Social scientists cannot hope to understand decision making if they do not analyze the organizational contexts and institutional frameworks in which there are conflicts of interest and the group and intergroup processes by which decisions are made.

Returning to the thoughts of Max Weber about types of organizations and bases of action, we can see that viewing the organization as the unit of analysis helps to dispel the fallacies of "individual rationality" and "maximization" of profits, outcomes, and rewards. Weber defined two types of rationality as bases of action: formal economic rationality and substantive value-rationality. Each is an ideal type. Formal rationality, based on the logic of means-ends relationships, is for Weber the most rare, and he classified economic activity by its degree of formal rationality.

Not all organizations (economic or otherwise) hold the goal of maximizing efficiency (e.g., charities and other types of human service organizations). Orthodox economic theory considers organizations that do not attempt to maximize efficiency suboptimal (inefficient) because of inappropriate resource allocation. In fact, these organizations do not maximize because the organization has goals other than to maximize efficiency. If we view suboptimality from the behavioral point of view and consider the market structure as one of several determining factors, the loci of efficiency and even decision making are not individuals, but organizations.

If the individual is no longer the unit of analysis and collectives are, we can more easily reject the neoclassical practices of emphasizing individuals and their rational decisions and concentrate on nonrational decisions of groups and organizations that are lodged in values and habit as well as means-ends relationships. For Weber, rational calculation of means-ends relationships that leads to greater efficiency is the exception; nonrational and inefficient actions are far more common. Since Weber, organizational theory has incorporated nonrational explanations based in a wide range of noneconomic values (substantive rationality), affect (emotions), and habit (tradition).

"Substantive rationality" is based in ethical, political, altruistic, and hedonistic values. Here, action may have little to do with economic "rationality" based on "opportunities for profit and on the success of profit-making activities" (Weber [1947] 1968:92). When values that cannot be measured entirely in economic terms are the bases of action, the organization's efficiency may be irrelevant. When values are measured in economic terms and formal rationality is found to reinforce substantive rationality, social values may be advanced. However, let us remember that this is the exception. Weber himself lays bare this contradiction in writing:

> No matter what the standards of value by which they are measured, the requirements of formal and of substantive rationality are always in principle in conflict no matter how numerous the individual cases in which they may coincide empirically. It is true that they may be made to coincide theoretically in all cases, but only under assumptions which are wholly unrealistic. (p. 191)

In addition to rational and normative bases of action, there is a third basis—emotion, the affectual base. Decisions made out of passion, fervor, or rage are not calculated, rational, means-ends-related decisions in the classical economic sense. Although these actions may have some economic consequences or may transmit some economic goods such as food or clothing, efficiency and profit concerns do not motivate the action. For example, parents may work to feed children out of love and affection, responsibility, and commitment, not out of a desire to maximize profit. This is not rational, calculative, maximizing action. Parents will work for salaries that are less than what is rational and far from maximizing in order to provide non-monetary bnenefits to their children.

Action based in tradition is not means-ends related. In the past, people may have acted on a rational basis, but now, these actions are based on habit, experience, and traditional ways in which the collective has always operated. These types of actions do not require calculations of means-ends relationships.

Weber posits calculative action based on formal rationality as unique, nonnormative, and precarious, with continual pressures to alter its form toward those based in absolute values, affect, and tradition. This makes the attempts of some social scientists to squeeze all types of behavior into the rational, maximizing mold quite amazing and exposes the ineffectiveness of such attempts.

Weber saw one type of organizational structure, the capitalistic bureaucracy, as the outgrowth of formal rationality. Rational-legal authority and logically consistent rules were two of the major characteristics of this type of organization. However, there are other types of organizations that rest on value rationality (such as public bureaucracies) and on mixes of action, such as emotions and value rationality (voluntary associations). In Weber's terms, attempts to explain decisions of these types of organizations solely through imposing rational choice logic are unsuccessful and unrealistic.

To summarize this point of the critique, decisions by and for organizations are distinctively different from decisions made by and for individuals. Group decisions replace the unitary decision maker. Groups of people make organizational decisions, and these groups have their own dynamics. Decisions are made through processes of negotiation (Strauss 1978), compromise, and bargaining and coalition formation (Bacharach and Lawler 1980). Decisions are not those that any single member of the organization would have made, or even the average (means). Organizational decisions are *political resultants* (Allison 1971). A wide array of organizational characteristics comes into play in organizational decision making—hierarchy (Granovetter 1985), specialization, centralization, communication networks (Hage 1974; Steinbruner 1974), and environments (Lawrence and Lorsch 1967). Organizations provide definable culture or value frames (Ouchi 1981) that influence decisions. Tasks, goals, and authority structures (Williamson 1987) affect premises, parameters, and content for organizational decision making. An integrated theory of organizations does not exist. Yet several authors have tried to list some of the core premises (Bacharach and Lawler 1980; Rosati 1981).

Similarly, Michael T. Hannan (1992) suggests decoupling the micro and macro levels and discusses issues involved in moving from the individual level to the organizational level to the societal level of analysis. Specifically, he suggests that rational action at the individual level need not result in rational action by the organization. Hannan (1992) argues that no theory of action is necessary to account for outcomes. Although I agree that rational action at the individual level, as defined by RCT, does not result in rational action by organizations, I do feel the need to understand the micro-macro links and dysfunctions.

Marini (1992) reaches different conclusions. She points out that models of purposive action consider the roles of social production and framing as connectors between social systems (groups) and individual actors and between individual actions and system outcomes. But she cautions against trying to bridge more than two levels. Thus, individual actions can be used only to explain actions at the group level. She concludes that one cannot predict macro-level actions (organizational, national, and international) from knowledge of individual actions. Richard Munch (1992b), in an excellent social critique of Coleman's *Foundations of Social Theory* (1990), argues that as rational actors choose the most beneficial way to act, they see relationships between macro- and microphenomena unidimensionally. Thus, he defines the relationships between macro- and microphenomena as more complex than the simpler connections envisioned by Coleman (1990).

9. ORGANIZATIONS FUNCTION RATIONALLY

The assumption that organizations are rational has developed several meanings. The term "rational organization" has been used to describe organizational functioning in which (1) means-ends relationships are assumed—certain structures and processes result in certain outcomes or performances, (2) organizational efficiency is maximized, and (3) decision making follows a certain form of logic considered more rational than others (Zey-Ferrell 1981).

As pointed out elsewhere (Zey-Ferrell 1981), these definitions often overlap such that achieving relationships between means and ends and making the organization more efficient are thought to occur simultaneously. Confusion occurs when efficient is not the most rational method of operating, and when the two terms are used synonymously (Albrow 1970). Furthermore, what is rational for one group of actors within the organization may not be rational for other groups or for the organization as a whole. Rational choice models assume that organizations are at least intended to be rational instruments in the pursuit of the goals of their owners, managers, or administrators. When nonrationality and irrationality occur, it is the function of managers and administrators to replace such actions with rational ones. The better and more rational the decisions, the more rational is the organization, and ultimately, the more efficient is the organization. Because of this characteristic, the rational choice model may be better understood as a rational model of administrative decision making. Administrative choices and decisions are the most highly valued. This is also the embeddedness argument. In actuality, what may occur when managers and administrators are trying to act rationally is a mapping out of conditions of the most efficient (rational) method of controlling the organization, which may have little to do with organizational means-ends relationships. It is often in contradiction to the goals of workers, labor management, and society as a whole and may not even lead to efficiency.

There is a litany of reasons that organizations are not totally rational instruments in pursuit of the dominant coalition's goals. Individual and organizational rationality are not the same. People who make up organizations do not always act rationally in the interest of the dominant coalition or the collective unit. If they do choose to act in the interest of the dominant coalition or in the interest of the collective good, they seldom have a consistent ordering of goals; they do not always pursue systematically the goals they do hold; there are inconsistencies of individual preferences and beliefs; they have incomplete information; they have an incomplete list of alternatives; they seldom conduct an exhaustive search of alternatives; and they do not always know the relationships between the organizational means and ends (March and Simon 1958; Zey-Ferrell 1981). Effective action in pursuit of goals is difficult and often impossible because of unexpected and uncertain events internal and external to the organization.

Because of the multiplicity of actors within the organization and the diversity of their goals, a multiplicity of rationalities exists within the organization. Occupational and organizational crimes impede the connections between means and ends of the organization (Katz 1988; Vaughan 1989; Zey 1991). In addition, ineptitude, inaction, negligence, and human error make the organization nonrational. Furthermore, there are "institutionalized myths" (Meyer and Rowan 1977) that contradict and compete with organizational efficiency and rationality.

10. ORGANIZATIONS FUNCTION EFFICIENTLY

Organizations provide an imperfect context in which to make decisions. Prior to the past two decades, organizational theorists assumed that organizational means and ends were connected regardless of type of organization, and recently, that certain environmental, technological, and other parameter variables are related to certain internal structures. More recently, these assumptions have come into question. Meyer and Rowan (1977) assume that, rather than connected means-ends relationships,

structural elements are often loosely linked to each other and to activities, rules are often violated, decisions are often unimplemented, or, if implemented, have uncertain consequences, technologies are of problematic efficiency, and evaluation systems are subverted or rendered so vague as to provide little coordination. (p. 342)

Karl E. Weick (1976) coined the term "loose coupling" to indicate that the links between organizational characteristics, between means and ends, and between structure and process are not as tight as rational theories would have us believe. Michael D. Cohen, James C. March, and Johan P. Olsen (1972) developed the "garbage can" model to describe the imperfect, inconsistent, nonrational organizational context of decision making (Zey-Ferrell 1981).

Rational choice models assume that the market economy is a separate system that is autonomous, self-contained, and self-regulating through perfect competition and laissez-faire principles. I argue that economy is but one subsystem among many in society—polity, economy, and cultural subsystems also influence decisions. Thus, social, political, and cultural embeddedness factors influence and explain the functioning of the economic system (Burk 1985; Fligstein 1990a, 1990b; Granovetter 1985; Zey 1991).

11. POWER AND CONFLICT ARE LIMITED

Munch (1992b) notes that Coleman's RCT contains a limited concept of power. It is either a structural condition within economic transactions, or it is shaped by economic calculations and transactions. The more unequal the power, the greater will be the gap between benefits for the superior and those for the inferior. The relationship persists because both parties are better off in it than out of it. Munch points out that this limited economic view of power does not consider its internal character (e.g., some parties cannot leave power relationships), normative structure, and symbolic effects.

RCT stipulates that authority results from a principal delegating authority to an agent, whose cooperation and trust benefits the principal. Munch argues that authority can also be based on physical coercion or democratic election. Those who fought (for and against) or voted (for and against) are subject to those who won or took office, respectively. In contrast to the tenets of RCT, the more powerful the victor or elected authority, the less the authority must exchange benefits for an individual's compliance.

RCT has difficulty explaining conflict because, when conceptualized as an economic transaction, both of the conflicting parties benefit from the relationship. Munch argues that in conflict relationships, one party's gain to a certain degree results in the other party's loss to the same degree. If parties cannot leave the relationship, they must face and resist each other—this is conflict.

I would like to conclude by quoting Bohman (1992):

> The limits of [RCT's] explanations show that it is an incomplete theory of social action and that it can remain vital only by incorporating other theories at different levels of explanation. RCT itself should remain narrow . . . if it is to retain its explanatory power. (p. 225)

Conclusion

There is a comfortable fit between economic theory and American culture. To trace all action back to individual rationality is to make it understandable within our peculiarly individualistic and rationalistic culture. At the same time, rational choice theorists escape all consideration of ethical claims by the individuals and organizations whose behavior they purport to predict and "explain." Quite simply, they uphold economic theory and America's own implicit moral order, or ideology, while claiming the universal applicability of their axioms. That moral order is, of course, an elegant, mathematical restatement of utilitarianism, a philosophy that fits American capitalism and the conservative political economy of the liberal economic order.

I disagree with Richard Hernstein (1990:356) that rational choice fails as a description of actual behavior, but *remains unequaled as a theory*. I argue that a theory must describe and explain reality, or it is inadequate. Because RCT is normative only, it is ineffective.

RCT acknowledges the limitation of time horizons, incomplete information, faulty knowledge, and limited capacity for understanding complexities, but it saves the model by covering its inadequacies. RCT survives counter evidence by placing no limits on implausibility or inconsistency of its inferred utilities and by appealing to the undeniable fact that organisms may calculate incorrectly, be ignorant, forget, or have limited time horizons. Rational choice ignores the evidence that organizations—which are not rational, unitary, self-interested beings—and not individuals, make most decisions. Do such actions result in the protection of a theory that in turn inhibits our understanding of human behavior? In that case, advocating RCT inhibits the advancement of theories that explain the real world.

I would recommend that we stop debating whether the neoclassical economic theory of formal rationality and utility maximization on which the rational choice models are based provides a necessary and sufficient foundation for explaining and predicting economic behavior or any other type of social choice. The evidence is overwhelming that it does not (Simon 1987; Kahneman et al. 1982).

Implications

We do our students a disservice by teaching them that the rational choice models of decision making are the only acceptable models. Students may perceive rational choice models not only as explanation, but also as justification for making decisions on rational bases only. That is, students may make not only economic decisions, but also family and personal relationship decisions on a rational, self-interested, even narcissistic basis. Simply put, studying the rational choice models exclusively may have a negative normative effect on our students. Students of rational choice may make decisions differently from other students. For example, Gerald Marwell and Ruth Ames (1981) found that graduate students in economics "free ride" more often than other students. Could it be that theories taught in economics prepare students to maximize their self-interest to the detriment of the collective? Carried to their extreme, rational choice models define competition as the core human value, and therefore, the higher the level of competition, the better for humans and collectives. According to this view, competition is the essential pleasure of life. If these are the values we teach, winning is the rational choice for all politics, and maximized wealth is the rational choice of all economic behavior. The political and economic implications of teaching only these theories may be less apparent than teaching more radical theories because the implications of teaching approaches to knowledge that reinforce the status quo are generally less noticeable. We may wish to consider whether more balanced perspectives may better predict action and may better depict the importance of ethical judgment (Solo 1981).

Note

1. This chapter has been adapted from the first chapter of Zey (1992).

References

Abell, Peter. 1992. "Is Rational Choice Theory a Rational Theory?" Pp. 183-206 in *Rational Choice Theory: Advocacy and Critique*, edited by James S. Coleman and Thomas J. Fararo. Newbury Park, CA: Sage.

Albrow, Martin. 1970. *Bureaucracy*. London: Macmillan.

Alchian, A. A. and S. Woodward. 1988. "The Firm Is Dead: Long Live the Firm." [Review of Oliver E. Williamson's *The Economic Institutions of Capitalism.*] *Journal of Economic Literature* 26:65-79.

Aldrich, Howard. 1979. *Organizations and Environments*. Englewood Cliffs, NJ: Prentice Hall.

Allison, Graham T. 1971. *Essence of Decision: Explaining the Cuban Missile Crisis*. Boston: Little, Brown.

Allison, Graham T. and Peter Szanton. 1976. "Public and Private Management: Are They Fundamentally Alike in All Unimportant Respects?" Pp. 184-99 in *Current Issues in Public Administration*, edited by F. Land. New York: St. Martin's.

Arendt, Hannah. 1963. *Eichmann in Jerusalem*. New York: Viking.

Arrow, Kenneth J. 1951. *Social Choice and Individual Values*. New Haven, CT: Yale University Press.

Arrow, K. and L. Hurwicz. 1972. "An Optimality Criterion for Decision-Making under Uncertainty." In *Uncertainty and Expectation in Economics*, edited by C. F. Carter and J. L. Ford. Clifton, NJ: Kelly.

Austin, J. L. 1975. *How to Do Things with Words*. 2d ed. Cambridge, MA: Harvard University Press.

115

Axelrod, R. and W. D. Hamilton. 1981. "The Emergence of Cooperation among Egoists." *American Political Science Review* 75:306-18.

Bacharach, Samuel B. and Edward J. Lawler. 1980. *Power and Politics in Organizations: The Social Psychology of Conflict, Coalitions, and Bargaining.* San Francisco: Jossey-Bass.

Baker, Wayne. 1983. "Floor Trading and Crowd Dynamics." Pp. 107-28 in *The Social Dynamics of Financial Markets,* edited by P. Adler and P. Adler. Greenwich, CT: JAI.

———. 1989. "The Social Structure of a National Securities Market." *American Journal of Sociology* 95:775-811.

Barnard, Chester. 1938. *The Functions of the Executive.* Cambridge, MA: Harvard University Press.

Barney, Jay B. 1990. "The Debate between Traditional Management Theory and Organizational Economics: Substantive Differences or Intergroup Conflict?" *Academy of Management Review* 15:382-93.

Barney, Jay B. and William G. Ouchi, eds. 1986. *Organizational Economics.* San Francisco: Jossey-Bass.

Bazerman, Max. 1986. *Judgment in Managerial Decisionmaking.* New York: John Wiley.

Becker, G. S. 1962. "Irrational Behavior and Economic Theory." *Journal of Political Economics* 70:1-13.

———. 1968. "Crime and Punishment: An Economic Approach." *Journal of Political Economics* 76:169-217.

———. 1975. *Human Capital.* New York: National Bureau of Economic Research.

———. 1976. *An Economic Approach to Human Behavior.* Chicago: University of Chicago Press.

———. 1981. *A Treatise on the Family.* Cambridge, MA: Harvard University Press.

Bendix, Reinhard. 1960. *Max Weber: An Intellectual Portrait.* Garden City, NY: Doubleday.

Bentham, Jeremy. [1841] 1983. *The Collected Works of Jeremy Bentham: Constitutional Code, Vol. 1.* Oxford, UK: Clarendon.

Berle, Adolph A., Jr. and Gardiner C. Means. 1932. *The Modern Corporation and Private Property.* New York: Commerce Clearing House.

Blau, Peter M. 1965. "The Comparative Study of Organizations." *Industrial and Labor Relations Review* 18(3):323.

———. 1970. "A Formal Theory of Differentiation in Organizations." *American Sociological Review* 35:201-18.

Blau, Peter M., Wolf V. Heydebrand, and Robert E. Stauffer. 1966. "The Structure of Small Bureaucracies." *American Sociological Review* 31:179-91.

Blau, Peter M. and Richard A. Schoenherr. 1971. *The Structure of Organizations.* New York: Basic Books.

Bower, Joseph. 1983. *The Two Faces of Management.* Boston: Houghton Mifflin.

Bohman, James. 1992. "The Limits of Rational Choice Explanation." Pp. 207-28 in *Rational Choice Theory: Advocacy and Critique,* edited by James S. Coleman and Thomas J. Fararo. Newbury Park, CA: Sage.

Buchanan, James M. and Gordon Tullock. 1962. *The Calculus of Consent.* Ann Arbor: University of Michigan Press.

Burk, James. 1985. "The Origins of Federal Securities Regulation: A Case Study in the Social Control of Finance." *Social Forces* 63:1010-29.

Camic, Charles. 1986. "The Matter of Habit." *American Journal of Sociology* 92:1039-87.

Caves, Richard E. 1980. "Industrial Organization, Corporate Strategy and Structure." *Journal of Economic Literature* 18:64-92.

Chandler, Alfred D. 1962. *Strategy and Structure: Chapters in the History of American Industrial Enterprise.* Cambridge: MIT Press.

————. 1977. *The Visible Hand: The Managerial Revolution in American Business.* Cambridge, MA: Belknap.

————. 1990a. "The Enduring Logic of Industrial Success." *Harvard Business Review* 67:434-41.

————. 1990b. *Scale and Scope.* Cambridge, MA: Belknap.

Child, John. 1972. "Organization Structure and Strategies of Control: A Replication of the Aston Studies." *Administrative Science Quarterly* 17(3):163-177.

Cohen, Michael D., James C. March, and Johan P. Olsen. 1972. "A Garbage Can Model of Organizational Choice." *Administrative Science Quarterly* 17:1-25.

Coleman, James S. 1984. "Introducing Social Structure into Economic Analysis." *American Economic Review* 74:84-88.

————. 1989. "The Paradigm of Rational Action." *Rationality & Society* 1:5-9.

————. 1990. *Foundations of Social Theory.* Cambridge, MA: Belknap.

————. 1992. "The Rational Reconstruction of Society." *American Sociological Review* 58:1-15.

Coleman, James S. and Thomas J. Fararo, eds. 1993. *Rational Choice Theory: Advocacy and Critique.* Newbury Park, CA: Sage.

Davidson, Donald. 1980. *Essays on Actions and Events.* Oxford, UK: Oxford University Press.

Debreu, Gerard. 1959. *Theory of Value: An Axiomatic Analysis of General Equilibrium.* New Haven, CT: Yale University Press.

Domhoff, G. W. 1970. *The Higher Circles: The Governing Class in America.* Englewood Cliffs, NJ: Prentice Hall.

————. 1974. *The Bohemian Grove and Other Retreats.* New York: Harper and Row.

————. 1978. *Who Really Rules? New Haven and Community Power Re-Examined.* New Brunswick, NJ: Transaction Books.

————. 1979. *The Powers That Be: Processes of Ruling Class Domination in America.* New York: Random House.

————. 1983. *Who Rules America Now? A View of the '80s.* Englewood Cliffs, NJ: Prentice Hall.

————. 1987. "Corporate Liberal Theory and the Social Security Act: A Chapter in the Sociology of Knowledge." *Politics and Society* 16:297-330.

————. 1990. *The Power Elite and the State: How Policy Is Made in America.* New York: Aldine de Gruyter.

Donaldson, Lex. 1985. *In Defense of Organization Theory: A Reply to the Critics.* New York: Cambridge University Press.

————. 1990a. "The Ethereal Hand: Organizational Economics and Management Theory." *Academy of Management Review* 15:369-81.

————. 1990b. "The Rational Basis for Criticisms of Organizational Economics: A Reply to Barney." *Academy of Management Review* 15:394-401.

————. 1995. *American Anti-Management Theories of Organization: A Critique of Paradigm Proliferation.* Cambridge, UK: Cambridge University Press.

Doucouliagos, C. 1994. "A Note on the Volution of Homo Economicus." *Journal of Economics Issues* 3:877-83.

Durkheim, Emile. [1890] 1973. "The Principles of 1789 and Sociology." Pp. 34-42 in *Emile Durkheim on Morality and Society,* edited by Robert Bellah. Chicago: University of Chicago Press.

————. [1905] 1977. *The Evolution of Educational Thought.* Translated by Peter Collins. London: Routledge & Kegan Paul.

————. [1895] 1982. *The Rules of Sociological Method.* Edited by Steven Lukes. Translated by W. D. Halls. New York: Free Press.

Edwards, Richard. 1979. *Contested Terrain: The Transformation of the Workplace in the Twentieth Century.* New York: Basic Books.

Edwards, Ward and Amos Tversky. 1967. *Decision Making: Selected Readings.* Middlesex, UK: Penguin.

Ehrlich, I. 1973. "Participation in Illegitimate Activities: A Theoretical and Empirical Investigation." *Journal of Political Economy* 81:521-65.

Einhorn, Hillel J. and Robin M. Hogarth. 1987. "Decision Making under Ambiguity." Pp. 41-66 in *Rational Choice: The Contrast Between Economics and Psychology,* edited by Robin M. Hogarth and Melvin W. Reder. Chicago: University of Chicago Press.

Elster, Jon. 1979. *Ulysses and the Sirens.* Cambridge, UK: Cambridge University Press.

————. 1983. *Sour Grapes.* Cambridge, UK: Cambridge University Press.

————. 1986. "Introduction." In *Rational Choice,* edited by Jon Elster. New York: New York University Press.

Etzioni, Amitai. 1986. "Mixed Scanning Revisited." *Public Administration Review* 38:8-14.

————. 1988. "Normative-Affective Factors: Toward a New Decision-Making Model." *Journal of Economic-Psychology* 9:125-50.

Fama, Eugene F. and Michael C. Jensen. 1983. "Separation of Ownership and Control." *Journal of Law and Economics* 26:301-26.

Fischoff, Baruch, Bernard Goitein, and Zur Shapira. 1981. "The Experienced Utility of Expected Utility Approaches." Pp. 315-39 in *Expectations and Actions,* edited by N. T. Feather. Hillsdale, NJ: Lawrence Erlbaum.

Flam, H. 1988. "Of Interest." *International Review of Sociology* 2:83-131.

————. 1990. "The Emotional Man and the Problem of Collective Action." *International Sociology* 51(1):39-56.

Fligstein, Neil. 1990a. "The Social Construction of Efficiency." Unpublished manuscript.

————. 1990b. *The Transformation of Corporate Control.* Cambridge, MA: Harvard University Press.

Frank, Robert H. 1990. "Patching Up the Rational Choice Model." In *Beyond the Marketplace: Rethinking Models of Economy and Society,* edited by Roger Friedland and A. F. Robertson. Chicago: Aldine.

————. 1994. *Microeconomics and Behavior.* New York: McGraw-Hill.

French, John R. P. and Bertram Raven. 1968. "The Bases of Social Power." Pp. 259-69 in *Group Dynamics*, 3d ed. Edited by Dorwin Cartwright and Alvin Zander. Evanston, IL: Row, Peterson.

Friedman, Deborah and Michael Hechter. 1988. "The Contribution of Rational Choice Theory to Macrosociological Research." *Sociological Theory* 6:201-18.

Friedman, Jeffrey, ed. 1996. *The Rational Choice Controversy: Economic Models of Politics Reconsidered*. New Haven, CT: Yale University Press.

Goetze, David and Peter Galderisi. 1989. "Explaining Collective Action with Rational Models." *Public Choice* 62:25-39.

Gordon, David. 1980. "Stages of Accumulation and Long Cycles." Pp. 9-45 in *Processes of the World System*, edited by T. Hopkins and I. Wallerstein. Beverly Hills, CA: Sage.

Gouldner, Alvin W. 1954. *Patterns of Industrial Bureaucracy*. Glencoe, IL: Free Press.

———. 1959. "Organizational Analysis." Pp. 400-428 in *Sociology Today*, edited by Robert K. Merton, Leonard Broom, and Leonard S. Cottrell, Jr. New York: Basic Books.

———. 1970. *The Coming Crisis of Western Sociology*. New York: Basic Books.

Granovetter, Mark. 1985. "Economic Action and Social Structure: The Problem of Embeddedness." *American Journal of Sociology* 91:481-510.

Green, Donald P. and Ian Shapiro. 1994. *Pathologies of Rational Choice Theory: A Critique of Applications in Political Science*. New Haven, CT: Yale University Press.

———. 1996. "Pathologies Revisited: Reflections on our Critics." Pp. 235-300 in *The Rational Choice Controversy*, edited by Jeffrey Friedman. New Haven, CT: Yale University Press.

Green, Leslie. 1981. "Authority and Public Goods." Paper presented at the annual meeting of the Canadian Political Science Association.

Hage, Jerald. 1974. *Communication and Organizational Control: Cybernetics in Health and Welfare Settings*. New York: Wiley Interscience.

Hage, Jerald and Michael Aiken. 1969. "Routine Technology, Social Structure, and Organization Goals." *Administrative Science Quarterly* 14:366-76.

Hall, Richard H. 1963. "The Concept of Bureaucracy: An Empirical Assessment." *American Journal of Sociology* 69:32-40.

———. 1968. "Some Organizational Considerations in the Professional-Organizational Relationship." *Administrative Science Quarterly* 12:461-78.

Hannan, Michael T. 1992. "Rationality and Robustness in Multilevel Systems." Pp. 120-36 in *Rational Choice Theory: Advocacy and Critique*, edited by James S. Coleman and Thomas J. Fararo. Newbury Park, CA: Sage.

Hannan, Michael T. and John H. Freeman. 1977. "The Population Ecology of Organizations." *American Journal of Sociology* 83:929-64.

Hardin, Russell. 1982. *Collective Action*. Baltimore, MD: Johns Hopkins University Press.

Harsanyi, John C. 1986. "Advances in Understanding Rational Behavior." In *Rational Choice*, edited by Jon Elster. New York: New York University Press.

Hausman, Daniel. 1992. *The Inexact and Separate Science of Economics*. Cambridge, UK: Cambridge University Press.

Hernstein, Richard J. 1990. "Rational Choice Theory: Necessary but Not Sufficient." *American Psychologist* 45:356-67.

Hesterly, William S., Julia Liebeskind, and Todd R. Zenger. 1990. "Organizational Economics: An Impending Revolution in Organization Theory?" *Academy of Management Review* 15:402-20.

Hickerson, Steven R. 1987. "Instrumental Valuation: The Normative Compass of Institutional Economics." *Journal of Economic Issues* 21:1117-43.

Hirsch, P., S. Michaels, and R. Friedman. 1987. " 'Dirty Hands' versus Clean Models.' " *Theory and Society* 16:317-36.

Hirschleifer, J. 1986. "Economics from a Biological Point of View." Pp. 319-71 in *Organizational Economics*, edited by J. Barney and W. G. Ouchi. San Francisco: Jossey-Bass.

Hirschman, A. 1985. "Against Parsimony: Three Easy Ways of Complicating Some Categories of Economic Discourse." *Economics and Philosophy* 1:7-21.

Hobbes, Thomas. [1651] 1966. *The English Works of Thomas Hobbes*, Vol. 3, *Leviathan*, edited by W. Molesworth. Aalen, Germany: Scientia.

———. [1651] 1968. *Leviathan*. Edited by C. B. Macpherson. Harmondsworth, UK: Penguin.

Holsti, O. R. 1979. "Theories of Crisis Decisionmaking." Pp. 99-139 in *Diplomacy: New Approaches in History, Theory, and Policy*, edited by P. G. Lauren. New York: Free Press.

Jensen, Hans E. 1987. "The Theory of Human Nature." *Journal of Economic Issues* 21:1039-74.

Jensen, Michael C. 1983. "Organization Theory and Methodology." *The Accounting Review* 58:319-37.

———. 1986. "Agency Costs of Free Cash Flow, Corporate Finance and Takeovers." *American Economic Review* 76:323-29.

———. 1988. "Takeovers: Their Causes and Consequences." *Journal of Economic Perspectives* 2(Winter):21-48.

———. 1989a. "Is Leveraged an Invitation to Bankruptcy? On the Contrary, It Keeps Shaky Firms Out of Court." *Wall Street Journal*, February 1, p. A14.

———. 1989b. "The Eclipse of the Public Corporation." *Harvard Business Review* 67:61-75.

———. 1993. "The Modern Industrial Revolution, Exit, and the Failure of Internal Control Systems." *Journal of Finance* 48:831-80.

Jensen, Michael C. and William H. Meckling. 1976. "Theory of the Firm: Managerial Behavior, Agency Costs and Ownership Structure." *Journal of Financial Economics* 3:305-60.

———. 1994. "The Nature of Man." *Journal of Applied Corporate Finance* 7(2):4-19.

Jensen, Michael C. and Kevin J. Murphy. 1990. "Performance Pay and Top Management Incentives." *Journal of Political Economy* 98:225-64.

Jensen, Michael C. and Richard S. Ruback. 1983. "The Market for Corporate Control." *Journal of Financial Economics* 11:5-50.

Kahneman, Daniel, Paul Slovic, and Amos Tversky, eds. 1982. *Judgement under Uncertainty: Heuristics and Biases*. Cambridge, UK: Cambridge University Press.

Kanter, Rosabeth Moss. 1972. *Commitment and Community*. Cambridge, MA: Harvard University Press.

Katz, Jack. 1988. *Seductions of Crime: Moral and Sensual Attractions in Doing Evil*. New York: HarperCollins.

Klappholz, Kurt. 1984. "Value Judgments and Economics." Pp. 276-92 in *The Philosophy of Economics: An Anthology*, edited by Daniel M. Hausman. Cambridge, UK: Cambridge University Press.

Knight, Jack. 1992. "Social Norms and Economic Institutions." *American Political Science Review* 86:1063-64.

Kuttner, Robert. 1985. "The Poverty of Economics." *Atlantic Monthly* (February):74-84.

Lane, Robert E. 1991. "Money Symbolism and Economic Rationality." Pp. 96-114 in *The Market Experience*. New York: Cambridge University Press.

Lawrence, Paul R. and Jay W. Lorsch. 1967. *Organization and Environment*. Boston: Harvard University, Division of Research, Graduate School of Business Administration.

Levi, Margaret, Karen S. Cook, Jodi A. O'Brien, and Howard Faye. 1990. "Introduction: The Limits of Rationality." Pp. 1-18 in *The Limits of Rationality*, edited by Karen Shweers Cook and Margaret Levi. Chicago: University of Chicago Press.

Luce, Duncan R. and Howard Raiffa. 1957. *Games and Decisions*. New York: John Wiley.

Mannheim, Karl. 1950. *Man and Society in an Age of Reconstruction*. Translated by Edward Shils. New York: Harcourt Brace Jovanovich.

Mansbridge, Jane J., ed. 1990a. "On the Relation of Altruism and Self-Interest." Pp. 133-43 in *Beyond Self-Interest*. Chicago: University of Chicago Press.

———, ed. 1990b. "The Rise and Fall of Self-Interest in the Explanation of Political Life." Pp. 3-22 in *Beyond Self-Interest*. Chicago: University of Chicago Press.

March, James and Herbert Simon. 1958. *Organizations*. New York: John Wiley.

Marini, Margaret Mooney. 1992. "The Role of Models of Purposive Action in Sociology." Pp. 21-48 in *Rational Choice Theory: Advocacy and Critique*, edited by James S. Coleman and Thomas J. Fararo. Newbury Park, CA: Sage.

Marwell, Gerald and Ruth Ames. 1981. "Economists Free Ride. Does Anyone Else? Experiments in the Provision of Public Goods." *Journal of Public Economics* 15:295-310.

Marx, Karl. [1867] 1977. *Capital*. Volume 1. New York: Vintage.

McKelvey, Richard M. and Howard Rosenthal. 1978. "Coalition Formation, Policy Distance, and the Theory of Games Without Sidepayments: An Application to the French *Apparentement* System." Pp. 405-50 in *Game Theory and Political Science*, edited by Peter C. Ordeshook. New York: New York University Press.

Merton, Robert. 1936. "The Unanticipated Consequences of Purposive Social Action." *American Sociological Review* 1:894-904.

Meyer, John and Brian Rowan. 1977. "Institutionalized Organizations: Formal Structure as Myth and Ceremony." *American Journal of Sociology* 83:440-63.

Mintz, Beth and Michael Schwartz. 1984. *The Structure of Power in the American Corporate System*. Chicago: University of Chicago Press.

———. 1985. *The Power Structure of American Business*. Chicago: University of Chicago Press.

Mizruchi, Mark S. 1982. *The American Corporate Network, 1904-1974*. Beverly Hills, CA: Sage.

———. 1989. "Similarity and Political Behavior among Large American Corporations." *American Journal of Sociology* 95:401-24.

Monroe, Kristen R. 1991a. "John Donne's People: Explaining Differences between Rational Actors and Altruists through Cognitive Frameworks." *Journal of Politics* 53:394-433.

———. 1991b. "The Theory of Rational Action: What Is It? How Useful Is It for Political Science?" Pp. 77-98 in *Political Science: Looking to the Future*, edited by William Crotty. Evanston, IL: Northwestern University Press.

Monroe, Kristen R., Michael C. Barton, and Ute Klingemann. 1990. "Altruism and the Theory of Rational Action: Rescuers of Jews in Nazi Europe." *Ethics* 101:103-22.

Munch, Richard. 1992a. "Rational Choice Theory: A Critical Assessment of Its Explanatory Power." Pp. 137-60 in *Rational Choice Theory: Advocacy and Critique*, edited by James S. Coleman and Thomas J. Fararo. Newbury Park, CA: Sage.

———. 1992b. *The Discourse of Sociological Theory*. Chicago: Nelson-Hall.

Myrdal, Gunnar. 1979. *Against the Stream: Critical Essays on Economics*. New York: Pantheon.

Olson, Mancur, Jr. [1965] 1971. *The Logic of Collective Action: Public Goods and the Theory of Groups*. Cambridge, MA: Harvard University Press.

Ordeshook, Peter C. 1993. "The Development of Contemporary Political Theory." Pp. 71-104 in *Political Economy: Institutions, Competition, and Representation*, edited by William A. Barnett, Melvin J. Hinich, and Norman J. Schofield. Cambridge, MA: Cambridge University Press.

Ouchi, William G. 1981. *Theory Z: How American Business Can Meet the Japanese Challenge*. Reading, MA: Addison-Wesley.

Pareto, Vilfredo. 1935. *The Mind and Society: A Treatise on General Sociology*. New York: Harcourt Brace Jovanovich.

Parsons, Talcott. 1947. "Introduction." Pp. 3-86 in *The Theory of Social and Economic Organization*, by Max Weber. Glencoe, IL: Free Press.

Parsons, Talcott and Edward A. Shils, eds. 1951. *Toward a General Theory of Action*. Cambridge, MA: Harvard University Press.

Pennings, Johannes. 1973. "Measure of Organizational Structure: A Methodological Note." *American Journal of Sociology* 79:688.

Perrow, Charles. 1981. "Markets, Hierarchies and Hegemony." Pp. 371-86, 403-404 in *Perspectives on Organization Design and Behavior*, edited by Andrew H. Van de Ven and William F. Joyce. New York: John Wiley.

———. 1986. *Complex Organizations: A Critical Essay*. New York: McGraw-Hill.

Pfeffer, Jeffrey. 1992. *Managing with Power: Politics and Influence in Organizations*. Boston: Harvard Business School Press.

Pitkin, Hanna Fenichel. 1972. *Wittgenstein and Justice: On the Significance of Ludwig Wittgenstein for Social and Political Thought*. Berkeley: University of California Press.

Pugh, D. S., D. J. Hickson, C. R. Hinings, and C. Turner. 1968. "Dimensions of Organization Structure." *Administrative Science Quarterly* 13:65-105.

Rawls, J. 1971. *A Theory of Justice*. Cambridge, MA: Harvard University Press.

Riker, William H. 1990. "Political Science and Rational Choice." Pp. 163-181 in *Perspectives on Positive Political Economy*, edited by James E. Alt and Kenneth A. Shepsle. Cambridge, UK: Cambridge University Press.

Rosati, J. A. 1981. "Developing a Systematic Decisionmaking Framework: Bureaucratic Politics in Perspective." *World Politics* 33:234-52.

Rousseau, Jean Jacques. 1762. *The Social Contract and Discourses*. Translated with an introduction by G. D. H. Cole. New York: E. P. Dutton.

Rubin, Paul H. 1983. Review of Nelson and Winter, "Toward an Evolutionary Theory of Economic Capabilities." *Journal of Political Economy* 91:718-20.

Samuels, Warren J. 1981. "The Historical Treatment of the Problem of Value Judgements: An Interpretation." Pp. 57-69 in *Value Judgement and Income Distribution*, edited by Robert A. Solo and Charles W. Anderson. New York: Praeger.

Satz, Debra and John Ferejohn. 1993. "Rational Choice and Social Theory." Stanford University, Stanford, CA. Unpublished manuscript.

Scheff, Thomas J. 1992. "Rationality and Emotion: Homage to Norbert Elias." Pp. 101-19 in *Rational Choice Theory: Advocacy and Critique*, edited by James S. Coleman and Thomas J. Fararo. Newbury Park, CA: Sage.

Schultze, Charles [Kuttner, Robert]. 1985. "The Poverty of Economics." *Atlantic Monthly* February:74-84.

Scott, W. Richard. 1981. *Organizations: Rational, Natural, and Open Systems*. Englewood Cliff, NJ: Prentice Hall.

Sen, A. M. 1973. "Behavior and the Concept of Preference." *Econometrica* 40:241-59.

———. 1977. "Rational Fools: A Critique of the Behavioral Assumptions of Economic Theory." *Philosophy and Public Affairs* 4:318-44.

Shapiro, Susan P. 1987. "The Social Control of Impersonal Trust." *American Journal of Sociology* 93:623-58.

Simon, Herbert A. 1957. *Administrative Behavior*. 2d ed. New York: Macmillan.

———. 1976. "From Substantive to Procedural Rationality." Pp. 129-48 in *Methods and Appraisal in Economics*, edited by J. Latsis. Cambridge, UK: Cambridge University Press.

———. 1979. "Rational Decision Making in Business Organizations." *American Economic Review* 69:493-513.

———. 1987. "Rationality in Psychology and Economics." Pp. 25-40 in *Rational Choice: The Contrast between Economics and Psychology*, edited by Robin M. Hogarth and Melvin W. Reder. Chicago: University of Chicago Press.

———. 1991. "Organizations and Markets." *Journal of Economic Perspectives* Spring:25-44.

Smith, Adam. [1776] 1979. *The Wealth of Nations*. New York: Random House.

Smith, Thomas Spence and R. Danforth Ross. 1978. "Cultural Controls on the Demography of Hierarchy: A Time-Series Analysis of Warfare and the Growth of the United States Army, 1960-1968." University of Rochester, Rochester, NY. Unpublished manuscript.

Solo, Robert. 1981. "Values and Judgements in the Discourse of the Social Sciences." Pp. 9-40 in *Values Judgements and Income Distribution*, edited by Robert A. Solo and Charles W. Anderson. New York: Praeger.

Steinbruner, J. D. 1974. *The Cybernetic Theory of Decision: New Dimensions in Political Analysis*. Princeton, NJ: Princeton University Press.

Stigler, George and Gary Becker. 1977. "De Gustibus Non Est Disputandum." *American Economic Review* 67:76-90.

Strauss, Anselm. 1978. "Summary, Implications, and Debate." Pp. 234-62 in *Negotiations: Varieties, Contexts, Processes, and Social Order*. San Francisco: Jossey-Bass.

Strom, Gerald S. 1990. *The Logic of Lawmaking: A Spatial Theory Approach*. Baltimore, MD: Johns Hopkins University Press.

Thompson, James. 1967. *Organizations in Action*. New York: McGraw-Hill.

Tool, Marc R. 1986. *Essays in Social Value Theory*. Armonk, NY: M. E. Sharpe.

Tversky, Amos and Daniel Kahneman. 1974. "Judgement under Uncertainty." *Science* 185:1124-31.

———. 1981. "The Framing of Decisions and the Psychology of Choice." *Science* 211:453-58.

———. 1987. "Rational Choice and the Framing of Decisions." Pp. 67-94 in *Rational Choice: The Contrast between Economics and Psychology*, edited by Robin M. Hogarth and Melvin W. Reder. Chicago: University of Chicago Press.

Udy, Stanley H., Jr. 1959a. "Bureaucracy and Rationality in Weber's Organization Theory." *American Sociological Review* 24:791-95.

———. 1959b. *Organization of Work*. New Haven, CT: Human Relations Area Files Press.

Ulen, Thomas S. 1983. "Review of Nelson and Winter." *Business History Review* 57:576-78.

Ullmann-Margalit, Edna. 1977. *The Emergence of Norms*. Oxford, UK: Clarendon.

Useem, Michael. 1984. *The Inner Circle: Large Corporations and the Rise of Business Political Activity in the U.S. and U.K.* New York: Oxford University Press.

———. 1993. *Executive Defense: Shareholder Power & Corporate Reorganization*. Cambridge, MA: Harvard University Press.

———. 1996. *Investor Capitalism: How Money Managers Are Changing the Face of Corporate America*. New York: Basic Books.

Vaughan, Diane. 1989. "Ethical Decision Making in Organizations: The Challenger Launch." Paper presented at the Conference on Organizational Deviance. Harvard University, Cambridge, MA.

von Neumann, J. and O. Morgenstern. 1947. *Theory of Games and Economic Behavior*. 2d ed. Princeton, NJ: Princeton University Press.

Wallace, Walter. 1980. *Sociological Theory and Introduction*. Chicago: Aldine.

Walsh, J. P. and J. K. Seward. 1990. "On the Efficiency of Internal and External Corporate Control Mechanisms." *Journal of Management Review* 15:421-58.

Weber, Max. [1920-21a] 1972a, [1920-21b] 1972b, [1920-21c] 1971. *Gesammelte Aufsätze zur Religionssoziologie*. 3 vols. Tubingen: Mohr Siebeck.

———. [1947] 1968. "Basic Sociological Terms." Pp. 3-62 in *Economy and Society*, Vol. 1. Edited by Guenther Roth and Claus Wittich. Berkeley: University of California Press.

Weick, Karl E. 1976. "Educational Organizations as Loosely Coupled Systems." *Administrative Science Quarterly* 12:1-11.

Wilber, Charles K. and Kenneth P. Jameson. 1983. *An Inquiry into the Poverty of Economics*. Notre Dame, IN: University of Notre Dame Press.

Willer, David. 1992. "The Principle of Rational Choice and the Problem of a Satisfactory Theory." Pp. 49-78 in *Rational Choice Theory: Advocacy and Critique*, edited by James S. Coleman and Thomas J. Fararo. Newbury Park, CA: Sage.

Williamson, Oliver E. 1970. *Corporate Control and Business Behavior: An Inquiry into the Effects of Organization Form on Enterprise Behavior*. Englewood Cliffs, NJ: Prentice Hall.

————. 1971. "Managerial Discretion, Organization Form, and the Multidivision Hypothesis." Pp. 343-86 in *The Corporate Economy: Growth, Competition and Innovative Potential*, edited by Robin Marris and Adrian Woods. Cambridge, MA: Harvard University Press.

————. 1975. *Markets and Hierarchies*. New York: Free Press.

————. 1981. "The Economics of Organization: The Transaction Cost Approach." *American Journal of Sociology* 87:548-77.

————. 1985. *The Economic Institution of Capitalism*. New York: Free Press.

————. 1987. *Antitrust Economics: Firms, Markets, Relational Contracting*. New York: Basil Blackwell.

Zald, Mayer. 1987. "The New Institutional Economics." *American Journal of Sociology* 93:701-708.

Zeitlin, Irving M. 1997. *Ideology and the Development of Sociological Theory*. 6th ed. Upper Saddle River, NJ: Prentice Hall.

Zeitlin, Maurice. 1974. "Corporate Ownership and Control: The Large Corporation and the Capitalist Class." *American Journal of Sociology* 80:1073-1119.

————, ed. 1980. "On Classes, Class Conflict and the State." Pp. 1-37 in *Class, Class Conflict, and the State*. Cambridge, MA: Winthrop.

Zey, Mary. 1991. "Reform of RICO: Legal versus Social Embeddedness Explanations." Paper presented at the 1991 annual meeting of the American Sociological Association, Cincinnati, OH.

————. 1992. *Decision Making: Alternatives to Rational Choice Models*. Newbury Park, CA: Sage.

————. 1993. *Banking on Fraud: Drexel, Junk Bonds, and Buyouts*. New York: Aldine de Gruyter.

————. 1994. Review of "Rational Choice Theory: Advocacy and Critique," edited by James Coleman and Thomas J. Fararo. *Social Forces* 77:273-75.

————. Forthcoming. "Embeddedness of Interorganizational Corporate Crime in the 1980s: Securities Fraud of Banks and Investment Banks." In *Research on the Sociology of Organizations*. Greenwich, CT: JAI.

————. Forthcoming. "The Transformation of Multidivisional Form." A Panel Analysis.

Zey, Mary and Brande Camp. 1996. "The Transformation from Multidivisional Form to Corporate Groups of Subsidiaries in the 1980s: Capital Crisis Theory." *Sociological Quarterly* 37:327-51.

Zey-Ferrell, Mary. 1979. *Dimensions of Organizations: Environment, Context, Structure, Process, and Performance*. Santa Monica: CA: Goodyear.

————. 1981. "Criticisms of the Dominant Perspectives on Organizations." *Sociological Quarterly* 22:181-205.

Author Index

Subject Index

Agency theory, 7, 37, 45-57, 63-64, 79
  agent/principal relationship, 45, 46
  autonomy/self determinacy, 14
Alternative behavior, 34, 66-68
  rationalized altruism, 67
Analysis:
  economic, 44, 88
  levels of, 5, 10, 42, 107
  organizational, 9, 10, 24, 30-31, 33,
    35, 47, 73, 78, 88, 103
  social behavior issues, 35, 37
  unit, 2, 8, 10, 14, 36, 80, 90, 103-104
Assumptions of rational choice:
  individuals antecedent, 90-91
  humans self-interested, 92-93
  humans only rational, 93-96
  humans maximize, 97-100
  utility is subjective, 100-101
  values are subjective, 96-97
  value neutrality, 101-103
Authority, 6, 39, 49, 53, 63-64, 69-70, 74-
  75, 106, 110
  and power, 49, 64, 74, 76
  delegation of, 48, 110

distribution of, 56
  Weber's topology, 75, 77, 84, 111
Autonomy, 11, 13, 75

Bank control theory, 49
Behavior, 70, 92, 104
  patterns, 14
Boundaries:
  perception of 67
  societal, 66
Bureaucracy, 73, 75, 76
  hierarchically organized, 63
  Weber's theory, 77, 106

Capital, 40, 46
Centralization, 106
Change, 24
  organizational, 42
  preferences and, 28, 92
  social, 5, 41, 42, 66, 69, 74, 82-93, 85,
    88, 91
Classical economic theory, 35
  neoclassical economic theory, 35
Classical management theory, 35

About the Author

Mary Zey is Professor of Economic Sociology and former head of the Department of Sociology at Texas A&M University, where she teaches and conducts research on organizations, especially industrial and financial corporations. In the past, she has studied such organizations as universities, volunteer organizations, and corporations. Her research focuses on the transformation of corporate form, control, mergers and acquisitions, and organizational crime. She is the author of *Dimensions of Organizations: Environment, Context, Structure, Process, Performance, Banking on Fraud;* and *The Transformation of Corporate Control, Strategy, and Structure, 1981-1995;* and editor of *Decision Making: Alternatives to Rational Choice Models, Complex Organizations: Critical Perspectives,* and *Readings on Dimensions of Organizations.* Her research on corporate structure form and strategy has been published in major sociological and business-related journals as well as *Research in the Sociology of Organizations.* Over the past two decades, she has collected a longitudinal database on the transformation of industrial and financial corporations from multidivisional to multisubsidiary managed corporations.